Introduction to costing

Tutorial

Aubrey Penning
David Cox
Michael Fardon

AAT WISE GUIDES – for convenient exam revision

This handy pocket-sized guide provides the **perfect study and revision resource** for the AAT Level 2 Certificate in Accounting.

available for:
 Bookkeeping 1
 Bookkeeping 2
 Working in Accounting and Finance
 Introduction to Costing

Visit www.osbornebooks.co.uk for further information and to place your order.

© David Cox, Michael Fardon, Aubrey Penning, 2013. Reprinted 2014, 2015.

All rights reserved. No part of this publication may be reproduced, stored in a retrieval system, or transmitted in any form or by any means, electronic, mechanical, photo-copying, recording or otherwise, without the prior consent of the copyright owners, or in accordance with the provisions of the Copyright, Designs and Patents Act 1988, or under the terms of any licence permitting limited copying issued by the Copyright Licensing Agency, Saffron House, 6-10 Kirby Street, London EC1N 8TS.

Published by Osborne Books Limited
Unit 1B Everoak Estate
Bromyard Road
Worcester WR2 5HP
Tel 01905 748071
Email books@osbornebooks.co.uk
Website www.osbornebooks.co.uk

Design by Laura Ingham

Printed by CPI Group (UK) Limited, Croydon, CR0 4YY, on environmentally friendly, acid-free paper from managed forests.

British Library Cataloguing in Publication Data
A catalogue record for this book is available from the British Library

ISBN 978 1909173 101

Contents

1	The costing system	2
2	Cost centres and cost behaviour	26
3	Inventory valuation and the manufacturing account	52
4	Labour costs	82
5	Providing information and using spreadsheets	100
	Answers to activities	129
	Index	151

Acknowledgements

The publisher wishes to thank the following for their help with the reading and production of the book: Maz Loton, Helen Pugh and Cathy Turner. Thanks are also due to Lynn Watkins for her technical editorial work and to Laura Ingham for her designs for this series.

The publisher is indebted to the Association of Accounting Technicians for its help and advice to our authors and editors during the preparation of this text.

Authors

Aubrey Penning has many years experience of teaching accountancy on a variety of courses in Worcester and Gwent. He is a Certified Accountant, and before his move into full-time teaching he worked for the health service, a housing association and a chemical supplier. Until recently he was the AAT course coordinator at Worcester College of Technology, specialising in the areas of management accounting and taxation.

David Cox has more than twenty years' experience teaching accountancy students over a wide range of levels. Formerly with the Management and Professional Studies Department at Worcester College of Technology, he now lectures on a freelance basis and carries out educational consultancy work in accountancy studies. He is author and joint author of a number of textbooks in the areas of accounting, finance and banking.

Michael Fardon has extensive teaching experience of a wide range of banking, business and accountancy courses at Worcester College of Technology. He now specialises in writing business and financial texts and is General Editor at Osborne Books. He is also an educational consultant and has worked extensively in the areas of vocational business curriculum development.

Introduction

what this book covers

This book has been written specifically to cover the 'Basic Costing' Unit which is mandatory for the revised (2013) AAT Level 2 Certificate in Accounting.

The book contains a clear text with worked examples and case studies, chapter summaries and key terms to help with revision. Each chapter has a wide range of activities, many in the style of the computer-based assessments used by AAT.

Osborne Workbooks

Osborne Workbooks contain practice material which helps students achieve success in their assessments. *Introduction to Costing Workbook* contains a number of paper-based 'fill in' practice exams in the style of the computer-based assessment. Please visit www.osbornebooks.co.uk for further details and access to our online shop.

1 The costing system

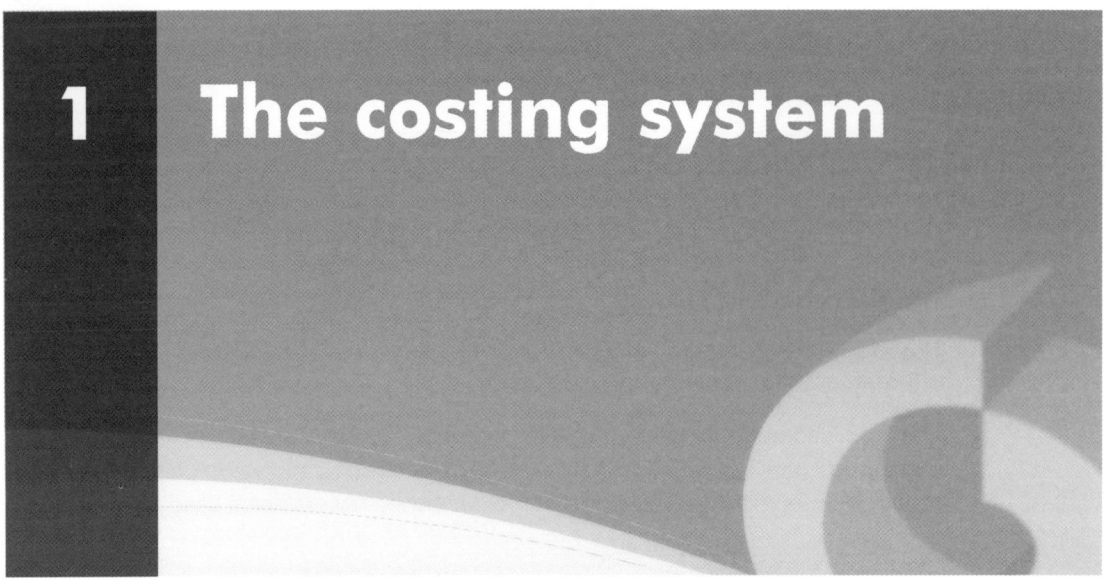

this chapter covers...

In this chapter we introduce costing by discussing what costing is, and then learn about some of the techniques that are used in costing.

We will start by explaining that the purpose of costing is to provide information for managers about costs and income in a range of organisations and situations. This will help managers to set selling prices, value inventory (stock), and make decisions.

We will then examine how costing systems are developed to match the organisation and its information needs. There are many different types of organisation, carrying out different activities in different ways, and the costing system needs to be able to produce the information that is most useful to manage the organisation.

Costing is part of management accounting and costing information is produced for those inside the business with a view to managing the future.

The next step is to see where the data that can be used for costing can be found. Calculations of current and future costs make use of the financial records (past 'historic' data) and also present day information and forecasts.

We will complete the chapter by showing how costs can be grouped together, or classified in several ways. The first is to divide costs into their elements – materials, labour and expenses. We can also classify costs based on their purpose or 'function', and by their 'nature'.

Once you have finished studying this chapter you should have a clear idea about why costing is needed, and appreciate some of the ideas that it uses.

PURPOSE OF COSTING

Costing (or 'cost accounting' to give its more formal name), enables the managers of a business to know the cost of the firm's output – whether a product or a service – and the revenues from sales. Once costing information is available, managers can use it to assist with decision making, planning for the future and the control of expenditure.

Cost accounting is widely used by:

- a **manufacturing business** which makes a product, eg a car
- a **business** that provides a service, eg a holiday company

A business – whether a manufacturer or a service provider – needs to keep its costs under review. In order to do this it needs accurate **cost information**. A cost accounting system will provide answers to questions such as:

What does it cost us to provide a student with a day's accountancy course?

What does it cost us to carry out a hip replacement operation?

What does it cost us to make a pair of trainers?

What does it cost us to serve a cheeseburger and fries?

What does it cost us to provide a week's holiday in the Canaries?

By being able to work out the cost of a product or service, the managers of an organisation can then use this cost to:

- help **determine a selling price** (which of course needs to be higher than cost in order to make a profit)
- **value inventory** (stock) that the organisation holds
- provide **information for financial statements**
- **make management decisions** (for example about how many items should be made and sold)

These are the key purposes of a costing system.

WHAT IS A COSTING SYSTEM?

A costing system is used by an organisation to collect information about costs and use that information for decision making, planning and control.

Every organisation can develop its own costing system to suit itself – what is important is the type of information it wants to get from the system, and this will determine how the system works. Costing systems could be:

- very simple – for example a series of written cost calculations for its products, or
- very complex – for example a computerised system that provides a range of reports that compare actual costs with expected costs and analyses the differences

The costing system that an organisation uses will need some 'rules' so that everyone using the system will do things in the same way. It would not be very useful if one product's cost was calculated in one way while another product's cost was worked out by an entirely different method. These 'rules' would be set up by the organisation – there are no legal or other external requirements that force organisations to carry out their costing in a particular way.

costing in different organisations

As already mentioned, costing systems will be different for different organisations. We have already seen that organisations as different as hospitals and holiday companies will need to have a costing system that suits their needs. We will show how a costing system divides up or classifies costs into various categories to make the information about costs more useful.

This **classification of costs** will also be different depending on the organisation and what it does, for example a hairdresser and a garage that sells cars.

FINANCIAL ACCOUNTING AND MANAGEMENT ACCOUNTING

Much of your accounting studies will be based on '**financial accounting**' where ledgers and other books and records are used to record financial transactions. If you study the basics of accounting you are likely to look first at bookkeeping. Although some of the information that is used in a costing system will come from the financial accounting ledgers, the costing system is usually quite separate, and has distinctly different purposes as we have already noted – to help with decision making, planning and control.

Costing is part of a larger area of study called '**management accounting**', which also includes topics such as budgeting and analysing the performance of a business or other organisation.

The following simple diagram (see next page) illustrates the relationship between financial and management accounting.

We will now examine the relationship between these two types of accounting in more detail.

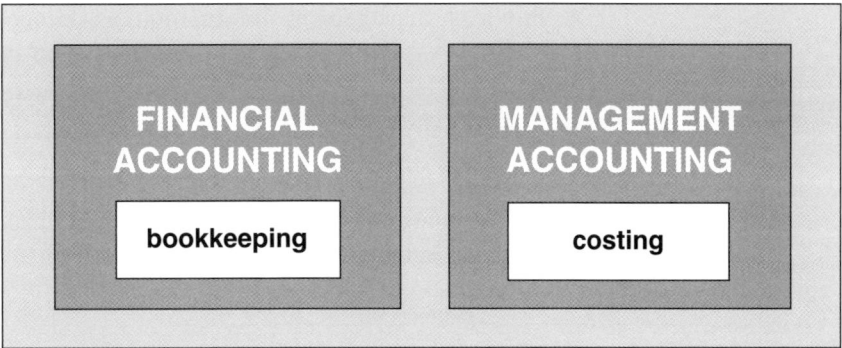

what is financial accounting?

Financial accounting is concerned with recording financial transactions that have happened already, and with providing information from the accounting records, for example, in order to prepare VAT returns, and the financial statements of a business.

The main features of financial accounting are that it:

- records transactions that have happened already
- looks back to show what has happened in the past
- is accurate to the nearest penny, with no estimated amounts
- is often a legal requirement to keep accounts (for example in order to prepare VAT returns)
- maintains confidentiality of information (eg payroll details, VAT returns)

what is management accounting?

Management accounting (including costing) is concerned with looking at actual transactions in different ways from financial accounting. In particular, the costs of each product or service are considered both in the past and as the likely costs in the future.

In this way, management accounting is able to provide information to help the business or organisation plan for the future.

The main features of management accounting are that it:

- uses accounting information to summarise transactions that have happened already and to make estimates for the future
- looks in detail at the costs and the sales income of products and services
- looks forward to show what is likely to happen in the future
- may use estimates where these are the most suitable form of information
- provides management with reports that are of use in running the business or organisation

- provides management information as frequently as circumstances demand – speed is often vital as information may go out-of-date very quickly
- is not usually sent to people outside the organisation – it is for internal use
- maintains confidentiality of information (eg payroll details)

A detailed summary of the differences between financial and cost accounting is illustrated in the diagram below.

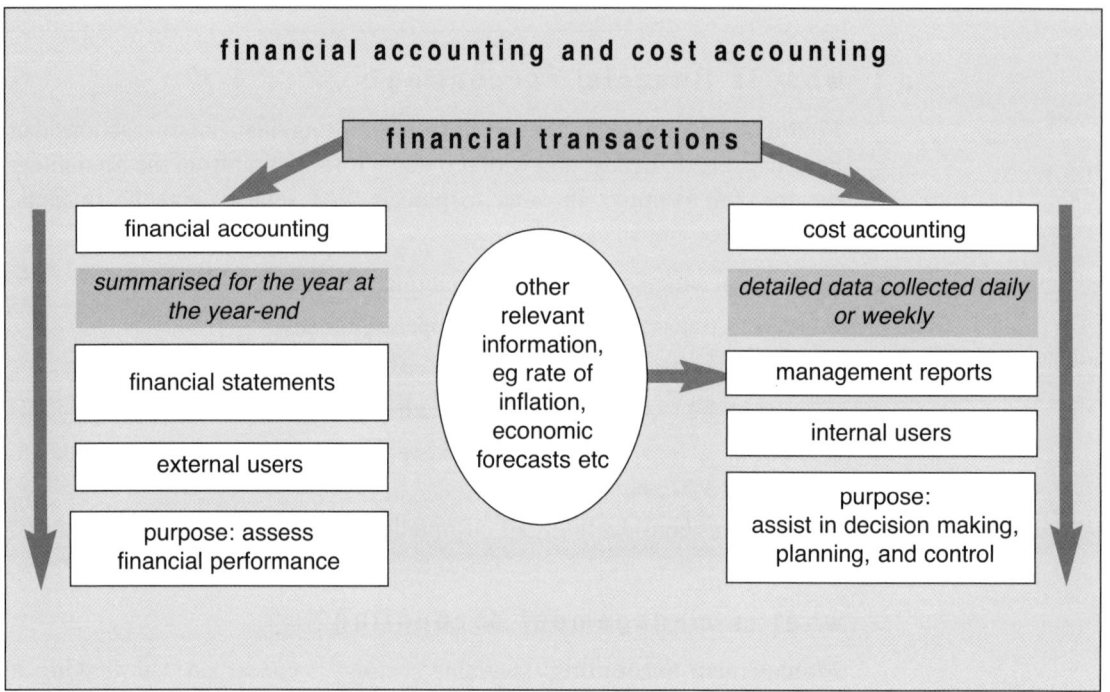

SOURCES OF DATA FOR COSTING

We saw in the last section how financial accounting has a different focus to costing, which is an important part of management accounting. While financial accounting keeps accurate records of what has already happened, costing goes beyond that to use various forms of information to determine current and future costs as well as monitor costs that have recently been incurred.

The **sources of data** for costing will include some of the data that is also used for financial accounting, but will also extend to a range of other sources that will help to provide useful information.

Costs can therefore be seen as being:

- from the past – these are known as **historic costs**
- relating to the present – these are known as **current costs**
- projections for the future – these are known as **future costs**

We will now explain these in more detail.

financial accounting data – historic costs

The majority of financial accounting data has come from entering in the bookkeeping ledgers items such as:

- invoices for sales and purchases
- payments
- receipts
- payroll

This provides an accurate record of what has already happened **in the past**. By examining the financial accounting records a business could find out, for example:

- how much was paid in rent last year
- what was the cost of paying wages last month
- how much was paid for materials in the last quarter

By looking beyond the ledger entries to the actual invoices and other financial accounting source documents a business could also find out in more detail, for example:

- how much the monthly rent was during each month of last year
- how many employees there were last month and how much each grade of labour was paid
- how much was charged by suppliers for specific materials, and what quantities were bought

At this level of detail the information is more useful for costing purposes, and we can see how it can be used to build up historic cost figures.

costing data – current and future costs

While financial accounting information, and the source documents of invoices and payroll provide accurate information about the **past** (including the recent past), we need to look at other sources so that we can calculate costs for the **current period** (the present time) and **future periods**. Not all the sources of data can be totally accurate, and businesses have to rely on estimates for some figures.

If a business needs to find the cost of materials or expenses, there may be:

- purchase orders (for goods or services ordered already) or
- quotations (for those that may be ordered later)

If the business wants to cost items further for the future, it may be necessary to approach possible suppliers for an estimate.

Where labour costs are concerned a business should be able to find out the current rates of pay and allow for any expected pay rises. If it is planning a new product, it should work out how long it will take to make that product. A business may have already prepared **financial forecasts** (**budgets**) in the past. These can provide a useful source of data for costs and income.

In Chapter 5 we will look in more detail at how we can provide information to managers based on data from various sources.

We will now use a short Case Study to help identify suitable sources of data for costing.

Case Study

ALLCOST LIMITED: SOURCES OF DATA FOR COSTING

situation

You are employed by Allcost Limited, a manufacturer of clothes for the fashion market. A trainee in the costing department has made the following suggestions. To help him with his training you have been asked to identify which statements are correct.

1. Forecasts (budgets) will always provide a good source of data for historic costs. ✗

2. When costing a future product the labour cost may need to be estimated by using planned labour rates and expected times to make the product. ✓

3. Forecasts (budgets) can provide a good source of data for future costs. ✓

4. A good source of data for historic costs are the financial accounting records and the documents that back up these records. ✓

5. If you have a firm quotation from a supplier this is a good source of data for current costs. ✓

6. The number of units that are planned for is not relevant for costing purposes. ✗

7. Payroll records which show how much people were paid and how long jobs took are a useful source of data for historic costs. ✓

8. The prices that the business plans to charge for its products are good sources of data for estimating future income. ✓

9. Agreements from suppliers about future prices will be used to help calculate future costs. ✓

10. Financial accounts provide the best source of data for future costs. ✗

required

You are to

(a) identify and list the statements that are correct

(b) point out and comment on the statements that are incorrect

solution

The following statements are **correct**:

2. When costing a future product the labour cost may need to be estimated by using planned labour rates and expected times to make the product.

3. Forecasts (budgets) can provide a good source of data for future costs.

4. A good source of data for historic costs are the financial accounting records and the documents that back up these records.

5. If you have a firm quotation from a supplier this is a good source of data for current costs.

7. Payroll records which show how much people were paid and how long jobs took are a useful source of data for historic costs.

8. The prices that the business plans to charge for its products are good sources of data for estimating future income.

9. Agreements from suppliers about future prices will be used to help calculate future costs.

The following statements are **incorrect**:

1. Forecasts (budgets) will always provide a good source of data for historic costs.

    Comment: forecasts (budgets) are produced from historic costs.

6. The number of units that are planned for is not relevant for costing purposes.

    Comment: costing is often based on the number of units produced.

10. Financial accounts provide the best source of data for future costs.

    Comment: financial accounts primarily provide data for financial accounting.

INTRODUCTION TO CLASSIFYING COSTS AND INCOME

Every part of an organisation incurs costs – eg administration costs and production costs – and some will generate income, eg from sales of products or services. The costing system will be able to supply management information about costs and income for each part of an organisation.

In this next section we will consider the main types of costs and income and then explain how they are analysed in relation to the different functions of the business or organisation.

the elements of cost

All businesses and organisations, whether they manufacture products or provide services, incur costs – these can be broken down into three **elements of cost**:

- materials
- labour
- expenses

Materials costs include the cost of:
- raw materials and components bought for use by a manufacturing business
- products bought for resale by a shop or a wholesaler
- service items or consumables, such as stationery, bought for use within a business or organisation

Materials range from sheet metal and plastics used in a car factory, computer chips and other components bought in by a computer manufacturer, tins of baked beans and other goods bought in by a supermarket, through to photocopying paper used in a college. Virtually all businesses and organisations incur materials costs. We will examine material costs in more detail in Chapter 3.

Labour costs refers to the payroll costs of all employees of the business or organisation. These costs include:
- wages paid to those who work on the production line of a manufacturing business
- wages and salaries paid to those who work for a manufacturing business but are not directly involved in the production line, eg supervisors, maintenance staff, office staff, sales people
- wages and salaries of those who work in the service industry, eg shops, banks, restaurants, accountants
- public sector wages, eg of central and local government employees

We will examine labour costs in more detail in Chapter 4.

Expenses is a term that refers to all other running costs of the business or organisation that cannot be included under the headings of materials and labour. Examples include rent, rates, heating, lighting, telephone, advertising, insurance, and so on.

The vast majority of expenses are also classified as **overheads** (see the next section).

income

The main source of income for the private sector is from the sale of products or services. There may also be other, smaller, amounts of income, eg interest received on bank balances, rental income if a part of the premises is let to a tenant, government grants and allowances for setting up a new business or buying new technology.

When we look at coding systems in the next chapter we will see how these elements of cost are used to record costs in a costing system.

CLASSIFICATION OF COSTS BY FUNCTION AND NATURE

As well as dividing costs into materials, labour and expenses, it is also useful to show **why the costs have been incurred** – what the costs help to achieve in the organisation.

This breakdown of costs is sometimes called '**functional**' as it links to the different sections (called '**functions**') of an organisation.

We will start by showing how this classification of costs works for a manufacturing organisation. Here the two main functions are generally carried out in:

- the factory – where goods are actually produced, and
- the warehouse and offices – where the support **functions** take place (eg administration, selling and distribution, and finance)

costs in the factory – production costs

The costs incurred in the factory are **production** costs. 'Production' is the **function** into which these costs are classified.

We can divide these production costs further, into:

- **direct** costs, and
- **indirect** costs (often called overheads)

This analysis is sometimes called **classification by nature**.

Direct costs are costs that can be identified directly with each unit of output.

Indirect costs cannot be identified directly with specific units of output.

The term 'unit of output' refers to products that a manufacturer makes or services that are provided by a service organisation.

In the following explanations we will use the example of a furniture manufacturer to illustrate what we mean. For a furniture manufacturer the units of output are the chairs and other items of furniture that are manufactured.

Remember that we also divide costs into materials, labour and expenses, so that we now have up to six types of production cost:

direct costs

- **direct materials** – the cost of the materials used to make the items produced – for example the cost of the wood used to make chairs in a furniture factory
- **direct labour** – the cost of paying the employees who carry out the production – for example the cost of paying the wages of workers making chairs in a furniture factory
- **direct expense**s – there are very few examples of direct expenses, so at this stage in your studies you can normally ignore this category of cost

The total of direct costs is also called the **prime cost.**

indirect production costs (production overheads)

- **indirect materials** – the cost of materials that cannot be directly linked to specific items produced – for example the cost of replacement saw blades used in the factory making furniture
- **indirect labour** – the cost of employing people in the factory who do not actually make the products – for example the cleaners and supervisors in a furniture factory
- **indirect expenses** – the other costs of running a factory – for example the costs of heating and lighting a furniture factory

The total of direct costs and indirect production costs is simply known as **total production costs**.

costs outside the factory – non-production costs

As well as costs relating to the factory (the production costs) that we have just discussed, there are also the costs that relate to the support functions that generally take place in the warehouse or offices. These are **non-production costs** and will always be indirect costs (**overheads**). These costs are still divided into materials, labour and expenses, just like other costs.

The non-production costs may be divided into the functions of:

- administration
- selling and distribution
- finance

classification of costs – a summary

Classification of costs can be confusing, so the following may be useful to help you remember the ways that we often classify costs.

Classification by **element**:
- materials
- labour
- expenses

Classification by **function**:
- production
- administration
- selling and distribution
- finance

Classification by **nature**:
- direct costs
- indirect costs

The diagram below combines these classifications of cost and gives some examples – again based on a furniture manufacturer.

CLASSIFICATION OF COSTS

	Production ('factory') costs		Non-production ('warehouse & office') costs		
	Production Direct Costs (total = prime cost)	*Production Indirect Costs (overheads)*	*Administration Indirect Costs (overheads)*	*Selling and Distribution Indirect Costs (overheads)*	*Finance Indirect Costs (overheads)*
MATERIALS	Wood to make tables	Oil for production machinery	Stationery	Packing materials	–
LABOUR	Assembly workers' wages	Production supervisors' wages	Administration staff wages	Salespeoples' wages	–
EXPENSES	–	Factory rent	Office rent	Advertising costs	Interest charges on loans
	Total Production Costs		Total Non-production Costs		
	TOTAL COSTS				

14 introduction to costing tutorial

When you have studied the diagram on the previous page, see how its principles are put into action in the Case Study which follows.

Case Study

SPORTCLASS LIMITED:
CLASSIFYING COSTS FOR A MANUFACTURER

situation

You work for Sportclass Limited, a company that manufactures a range of sports equipment. The following list of costs has been compiled from the company records.

You have been asked to classify these costs in a table to illustrate to a new trainee how the company costing system works.

list of costs:

- Factory insurance   *IC - Expenses*
- Wages of employee who strings tennis racquets
- Wood used to make cricket bats
- Advertising costs
- Wages of employee who maintains production machines in the factory
- Bank overdraft interest
- Cost of telephone calls in administration department
- Wages of delivery driver
- Floor cleaning fluid for use in the factory
- Wages of office worker in administration department
- Stationery used in administration office
- Fuel for delivery van

solution

The table on the next page shows these costs inserted in the appropriate place according to the classification of the relevant cost.

	Production ('factory') costs		Non-production ('warehouse & office') costs		
	Production *Direct Costs*	*Production* *Indirect Costs*	*Administration* *Indirect Costs*	*Selling and* *Distribution* *Indirect Costs*	*Finance* *Indirect Costs*
MATERIALS	Wood used to make cricket bats	Floor cleaning fluid for use in the factory	Stationery used in administration office	Fuel for delivery van	–
LABOUR	Wages of employee who strings tennis racquets	Wages of employee who maintains production machines in the factory	Wages of office worker in administration department	Wages of delivery driver	–
EXPENSES	–	Factory insurance	Cost of telephone calls in administration department	Advertising costs	Bank overdraft interest

COSTS IN NON-MANUFACTURING ORGANISATIONS

So far we have used the manufacturing industry to illustrate the way that costs can be classified by element (materials, labour and expenses) and by function (production and non-production). The same principles apply to the classification of costs in non-manufacturing organisations – businesses that provide services, for example – although the classification by function will not include 'production' in these circumstances.

Some of the costs in non-manufacturing organisations can be identified directly with the units of output, so the analysis into **direct** and **indirect costs** is still valid. For example, a bus company's units of output are passenger journeys, so direct costs would include fuel for the vehicles and the wages of the bus driver, while indirect costs would include maintaining and cleaning the buses.

The tables on the next page show how costs could be classified in a variety of non-manufacturing organisations, both into direct and indirect costs, and also into materials, labour and expenses.

The non-manufacturing organisations shown below are a hairdresser, an airline, a refuse collection company and a theme park. **Classification** in the first table is by **element** (material, labour, expense) and in the second by **nature** (direct and indirect costs).

classification by element

ORGANISATION	COST	Material	Labour	Expense
hairdresser	Shampoo	✔		
	Stylists' wages		✔	
	Receptionists' wages		✔	
	Electricity			✔
airline	Aircraft fuel	✔		
	Pilots' wages		✔	
	Airport landing fees			✔
	Advertising			✔
refuse collection	Fuel for vehicles	✔		
	Supervisors' wages		✔	
	Operatives' wages		✔	
	Insurance			✔
theme park	Insurance			✔
	Ride staff wages		✔	
	Power for rides			✔
	Cleaning staff wages		✔	

classification by nature

ORGANISATION	COST	Direct	Indirect
hairdresser	Shampoo	✔	
	Stylists' wages	✔	
	Receptionists' wages		✔
	Electricity		✔
airline	Aircraft fuel	✔	
	Pilots' wages	✔	
	Airport landing fees	✔	
	Advertising		✔
refuse collection	Fuel for vehicles	✔	
	Supervisors' wages		✔
	Operatives' wages	✔	
	Insurance		✔
theme park	Insurance		✔
	Ride staff wages	✔	
	Power for rides	✔	
	Cleaning staff wages		✔

Case Study

ALBION RESTAURANT: COST CLASSIFICATION

situation

Albion Restaurant is a large restaurant. Some of the costs incurred by Albion Restaurant are as follows:

(a) wages of the cleaner
(b) cost of heating the restaurant
(c) wages of the chefs
(d) telephone charges
(e) paper table covers and napkins
(f) cost of ingredients for meals
(g) cleaning materials
(h) advertising costs
(i) maintenance contract for ovens
(j) wages of waiters and waitresses

required

You are an accounts assistant at Albion Restaurant. You are required to classify the above costs into the six categories shown in the table below. Give your answer by entering the costs into the table.

	DIRECT COSTS	INDIRECT COSTS
MATERIALS	cost of ingredients for meals	cleaning materials paper table covers & napkins
LABOUR	~~wages for cleaner~~ wages for chefs wages for waiters & waitress	wages for cleaner
EXPENSES		cost of heating the restaurant telephone charges advertising costs maintenance contract for ovens

solution

You classify the costs as follows:

	DIRECT COSTS	INDIRECT COSTS
MATERIALS	(f) cost of ingredients for meals	(e) paper table covers and napkins (g) cleaning materials
LABOUR	(c) wages of the chefs (j) wages of waiters and waitresses*	(a) wages of the cleaner
EXPENSES		(b) cost of heating the restaurant (d) telephone charges (h) advertising costs (i) maintenance contract for ovens

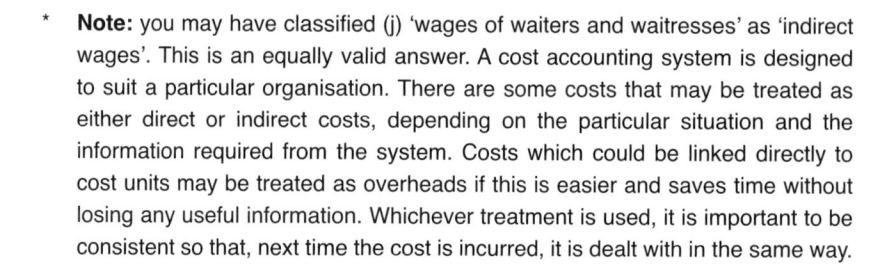

* **Note:** you may have classified (j) 'wages of waiters and waitresses' as 'indirect wages'. This is an equally valid answer. A cost accounting system is designed to suit a particular organisation. There are some costs that may be treated as either direct or indirect costs, depending on the particular situation and the information required from the system. Costs which could be linked directly to cost units may be treated as overheads if this is easier and saves time without losing any useful information. Whichever treatment is used, it is important to be consistent so that, next time the cost is incurred, it is dealt with in the same way.

an alternative classification

Since expenses are usually also classified as overheads (indirect costs) you could alternatively be asked to analyse costs into 'materials, labour, and overheads'. In this type of task you should assume that 'overheads' excludes materials and labour costs. An example of this is Activity 1.6 on page 22.

the next step – coding

Once costs and income have been classified we need to use a convenient method of keeping all the data together in a logical system. One way that is often used is a **coding system**, and in the next chapter we will examine how such systems can work.

Chapter Summary

- Costing provides information on the costs and income that arise from an organisation's products or services. Costing can help managers with decision making, planning and control.

- A costing system will be designed with the needs of the organisation in mind. There is no 'one size fits all' approach, so the system can be as simple or as complex as the managers require.

- Costing is part of the area of accounting called 'management accounting'. It concentrates on providing internal information about the future in a form that is useful and has no externally set rules that must be followed.

- There is a variety of sources of data within the organisation for costing, as well as some useful external sources. The data used will depend on whether the information required is for historic, current or future periods.

- Costs can be classified into the elements of materials, labour and expenses, and also by nature into direct costs and indirect costs (overheads). There are also functional classifications, the most common being production, administration, selling and distribution, and finance.

Key Terms

costing system — the system that an organisation has developed to collect information about costs and income so that it can be used to help with decision making, planning and control

management accounting — the area of accounting that includes costing: it concentrates on providing internal information about the future in a form that is useful; it has no externally set rules that must be followed

financial accounting — the area of accounting that includes book-keeping; it concentrates on providing historic information that can be used internally and also provided to external parties

budget — a future plan for an organisation, showing all the detail in financial terms; it is usually made up of various individual budgets

cost classification by element — grouping costs together according to the type of cost based on three categories – materials, labour and expenses (overheads)

cost classification by nature — grouping costs together according to whether they are direct costs or indirect costs

direct costs — costs that are directly identified with the units of output (the products or services that the organisation makes or provides)

prime cost — a term relating to the total of direct costs; it is often used to describe the total direct cost for a unit of output

indirect costs (overheads) — costs that are not directly identified with the units of output; these costs are divided into production and non-production costs in a manufacturing organisation

cost of production — a term relating to the total of direct costs and indirect production costs (production overheads)

Activities

1.1 Which one of the following statements is true?

(a) Financial accounting includes costing; management accounting includes bookkeeping

(b) Costing includes management accounting; bookkeeping includes financial accounting ✗

(c) Management accounting includes financial accounting; costing includes bookkeeping

(d) Financial accounting includes bookkeeping; management accounting includes costing ✓

Answer (a) or (b) or (c) or (d)

1.2 Which one of the following is a characteristic of financial accounting?

(a) Its purpose is to provide information for managers

(b) It is based on future events

(c) Its purpose is to provide information for owners and investors ✓

(d) The timing and content of its reports is decided by managers

Answer (a) or (b) or (c) or (d)

1.3 Which one of the following is a characteristic of management accounting?

(a) It is based on future events ✓

(b) It provides information for people outside the business

(c) It is based on past events

(d) It complies with company law and accounting rules

Answer (a) or (b) or (c) or (d)

1.4 Identify the following statements as being true or false by putting a tick in the relevant column of the table below.

	True	False
• Management accounting must comply with company law		✓
• Financial accounting provides information for owners and investors	✓	
• Management accounting is based on future events	✓	✗
• Financial accounting only provides information about what may happen in the future		✓

1.5 From the following table indicate two characteristics of financial accounting and two characteristics of management accounting by putting a tick in the relevant column.

Characteristic	Financial Accounting	Management Accounting
• It is based on future events		✓
• Its purpose is to provide information for managers		✓
• It complies with accounting rules	✓	
• It is based on past events	✓	

1.6 Severn Manufacturing Limited makes chairs for school and college use. The chairs have plastic seats, and tubular steel legs. You are to classify the following costs by by putting a tick in the relevant column of the table below.

Cost	Material	Labour	Overheads
Tubular steel	✓		
Wages of employee operating the moulding machine which produces the chair seats		✓	
Rates of factory			✓
Travel expenses of sales staff			✓
Plastic for making chair seats	✓		
Factory heating and lighting			✓

1.7 Crusty Limited is in business as a bakers.

Classify the following costs by nature (direct or indirect) by putting a tick in the relevant column of the table below.

Cost	Direct	Indirect
• Flour used to bake bread	✓	
• Rent of bakery		✓
• Wages of bakers	✓	
• Repairs to baking machinery		✓
• Currants used in buns	✓	
• Wages of bakery cleaner		✓
• Insurance of bakery		✓
• Salary of production manager		✓

1.8 Wyvern Water Limited bottles natural spring water at its plant at Walcoll at the base of the Wyvern Hills.

You are working in the costing section of Wyvern Water and are asked to classify the following costs by function (production, administration, or selling and distribution) by putting a tick in the relevant column of the table below.

Cost	Production	Administration	Selling and distribution
Wages of employees working on the bottling line	✓		
Insurance of delivery lorries			✓
Cost of bottles	✓		
Safety goggles for bottling line employees	✓		
Advertisement for new employees		✓	
Depreciation of bottling machinery	✓		
Depreciation of sales staff's cars			✓
Attendance at a trade exhibition			✓
Office heating and lighting		✓	
Sales staff salaries			✓

1.9 First Office Ltd manufactures a range of office furniture. The following list of costs has been compiled from the company records. You have been asked to classify these costs into a table to illustrate to a new trainee how the company costing system works.

List of costs

1. factory rent
2. wages of employee who makes desk legs
3. steel used to make desk legs
4. costs of sending out advertising brochure
5. wages of employee who maintains production machines in the factory
6. bank loan interest
7. cost of photocopier maintenance contract in administration department
8. wages of fork lift truck driver in warehouse
9. machinery oil for use in the factory
10. wages of accounts assistant in administration department
11. stationery used in payroll office (part of administration)
12. fuel for fork lift truck in warehouse

Required

Complete the table shown below by inserting the number of each of the costs on the list in the appropriate place.

	Production ('factory') costs		Non-production ('warehouse & office') costs		
	Direct Costs	Indirect Costs	Administration Indirect Costs	Selling and Distribution Indirect Costs	Finance Indirect Costs
MATERIALS	3	~~12~~ 9	11	~~11~~ 12	
LABOUR	2 ~~5~~	~~8~~ 5	10	~~10~~ 8	
EXPENSES		1	7	4	6

1.10 You are employed by Allsauce Limited, a manufacturer of table sauces.

A trainee in the costing department has made the following statements.

To help him with his training you have been asked to identify which of the following statements are true and which are false by putting a tick in the relevant column of the table below.

	True	False
• Budgets can never be used as a source of data for historic costs.	✓	
• Information to help with future costs can come from inside and outside the organisation.	✓	
• Future costs are impossible to estimate.		✓
• Financial accounting records and the documents that back up these records are a good source of data for historic costs.	✓	
• If you have a firm quotation from a supplier this is a good source of data for current costs.	✓	
• The number of products that the business forecasts to sell is a good source of data for estimating future income.	✓	✓✗
• Costing can only be used for manufacturing businesses, not the service industry.		✓ ✓
• Financial accounts can provide a reliable source of data for future costs.	✓✗	
• When costing a future product the labour cost may need to be estimated by using planned labour rates and expected times to make the product.	✓	
• The production level that is planned for is not relevant for costing purposes.		✓

2 Cost centres and cost behaviour

this chapter covers...

In this chapter we look in more detail at how the basic principles of costing that we explained in the last chapter are used in a costing system.

We will start by describing 'cost centres'. These are sections of the organisation that costs can be charged to and we will use the idea of 'functional' analysis (ie different areas of the organisation) that we examined in Chapter 1.

We will also examine 'profit centres' and 'investment centres', and see how they differ from 'cost centres'.

Next we will introduce the idea of coding systems by first identifying the three main types of coding that are used in costing. We will then use the various forms of classification of costs that we have already studied to see how costs could be analysed and coded to help with costing.

The third main topic covered in this chapter is 'cost behaviour'. This term relates to the way that costs react to changes in output or activity levels. Some costs remain the same in total ('fixed' costs), others change directly with changes in output ('variable' costs), while others contain an element of each of these behaviours ('semi-variable' costs).

We will learn about the features of these different cost behaviours, and will be able to identify the behaviour of a variety of costs for different organisations. We will then see how this knowledge of cost behaviour can be used to help calculate total costs and unit costs in a range of situations.

COST CENTRES

In Chapter 1 we saw that costs can be analysed by **function** into the main operational areas of an organisation, eg the functions of production, administration, selling and distribution, and finance. **Cost centres** are used to help with this functional analysis of costs.

Cost centres are sections of an organisation to which costs can be charged.

Cost centres may be based on the same functions that we have already described, or very often are based on dividing those functions up in a way that is more useful for the organisation. Thus a cost centre can be any function or section of the organisation. In a **manufacturing** business it can be an entire factory, a department of a factory, or a particular stage in the production process.

In a **service** industry it can be a shop, or group of shops in an area, a teaching department or a resources centre within a college, a ward or operating theatre in a hospital. Any section of a business can be a cost centre – based on what is most useful for the organisation's costing system. A manager or supervisor will be responsible for each cost centre and it is this person who will be taking data from the accounts system.

analysis of costs to different cost centres

When the cost centres have been established it is necessary to ensure that the accounts system is able to provide information to the manager of each cost centre. In order to do this, separate accounts are established for each cost centre to cover the main cost headings. For example, labour costs can be split between 'wages and salaries: production', 'wages and salaries: administration', 'wages and salaries: selling and distribution', and so on.

By analysing costs in this way the accounts system is able to provide the cost centre manager with information about how much has been spent by, or charged to, the centre over the last month, quarter, half-year, or year. This information will help the manager:

- to **plan for the future**, eg by using actual costs, he/she will be able to forecast next year's costs
- to **make decisions**, eg by comparing the costs of different products or services, eg whether to increase or decrease output
- **control costs**, eg by comparing actual costs with budgeted costs (see Chapter 5), he/she will be able to take steps to reduce costs

In this way the accounts system is able to tell the manager what has happened in each functional area in terms of financial information.

where does the information come from?

The sources of information for the analysis of costs include:

- purchase orders and purchase invoices, for materials and expenses costs
- payroll schedules, for labour costs
- bills and cash receipts, for expenses costs

The amounts of each cost are then analysed to the cost centre which has incurred the cost. The diagram below shows how this process works. A firm's policy manual should give details of which costs are to be charged to which cost centre.

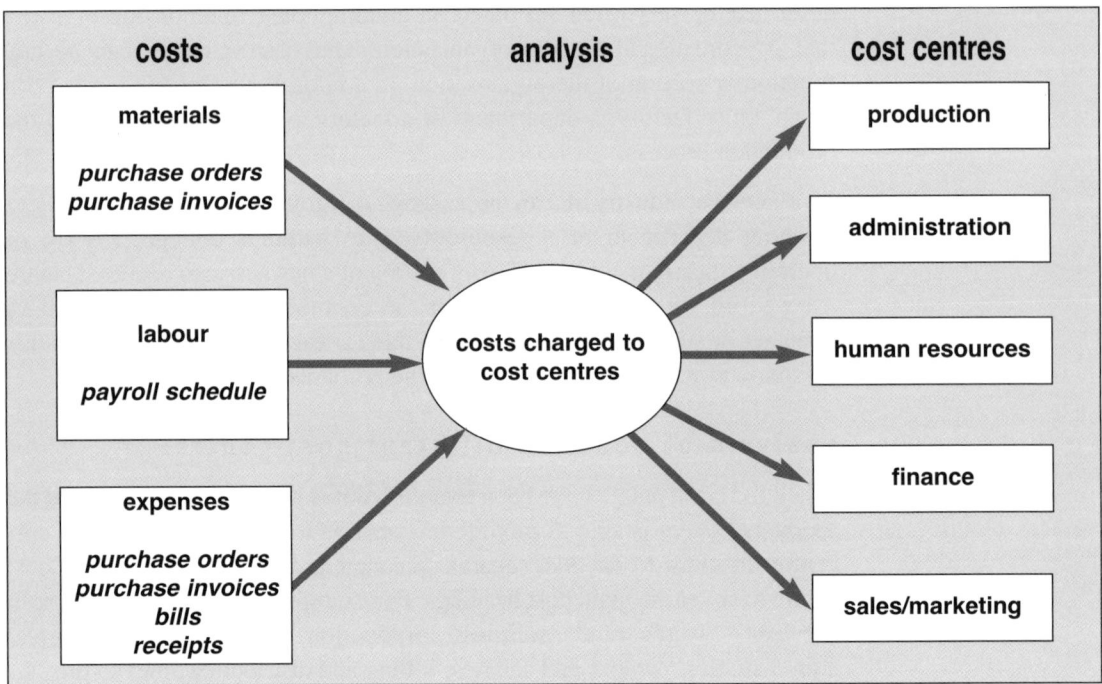

PROFIT CENTRES

For some sections of businesses the cost centre approach of analysing costs is taken to a further level by also analysing sales **income** to centres. As sales income less costs equals profit, such centres are called **profit centres**. Note that the source of information on sales comes from sales orders and sales invoices.

Profit centres are sections of a business to which costs can be charged, income can be identified, and profit can be calculated.

From the definition we can see that profit centres have both costs and income. It follows, therefore, that profit centres will be based on sections of the business that make products or services (incur costs) and sell them to customers (receive income from sales). For example, a clothing manufacturer might have 'dresses' as a profit centre, as shown in the following diagram:

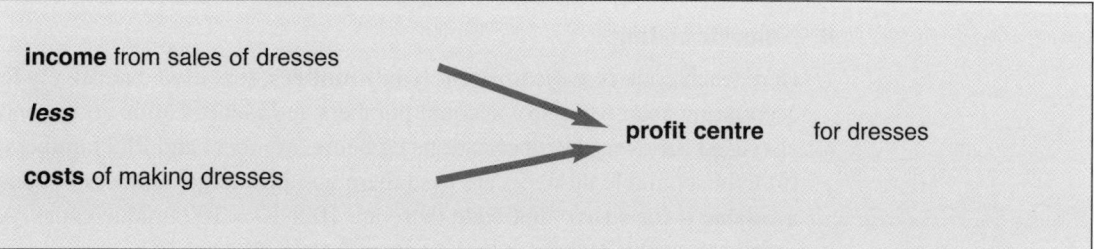

Note that many cost centres provide support services within a business or organisation and, so, cannot become profit centres because they do not have any significant income. For example, the administration department of a business is a cost centre to which costs can be charged, but it does not receive any income. As we have seen profit centres both incur costs and generate income.

Managers of profit centres will be getting information from the accounting system about the costs incurred and the income generated by their centre. By deducting costs from income they can calculate the profit made and can make comparisons with previous periods (eg last month, last quarter, last year, etc) and also with other profit centres (eg 'our profit was higher than yours last month').

INVESTMENT CENTRES

Investment centres are sections of the organisation where not only can information on income and costs be gathered, but also information on the amount of investment. Investment could take the form of non-current (fixed) assets (for example, buildings or machinery), as well as inventory and other current assets.

In this way the performance of the investment centre can be measured not just by the level of profit (as in a profit centre), but also by comparing the profit with the amount invested in that part of the business. An investment centre can therefore be like a mini business within the main business. An example of an investment centre could be an individual shop within a chain of shops operated by the same company.

CODING SYSTEMS

Coding systems are used to organise and analyse data. Coding systems are used extensively in costing, and are also used in many other situations. There are three main types of coding system that we must be able to identify and explain.

- **Numeric coding**

    Here, each code is made up entirely of **numbers**. It is used extensively in accounting and costing for account numbers and identification codes, and also used for everyday applications eg phone numbers and PIN numbers. If all the available numbers are used there will be a large number of codes available – for a two digit code there are 10 x 10 = 100 unique codes. A drawback of this system is that a numeric code may easily be forgotten.

- **Alphabetic coding**

    Each alphabetic code is made up entirely of **letters**. Many website addresses are really alphabetic codes, eg www.osbornebooks.co.uk. An alphabetic code has the advantage of being easier to remember than numbers if the 'words' created make sense, and can also provide many more available codes than numeric ones. For example, even for two letter codes from aa to zz there are 26 x 26 = 676 unique codes.

- **Alpha-numeric coding**

    This type of code is made up of both **letters and numbers**. A UK postcode is an example of alpha-numeric coding. Here the first two letters represent the main location (eg WR for Worcester) which helps the user. Some accounting systems use alpha-numeric coding for customer accounts, for example A01 to A99 for customers whose names begin with A, or CAM001 for a customer whose name begins with 'CAM', eg Cameron, Campion, Camus. These, like postcodes, are relatively easy to remember.

USE OF CODING IN COSTING

Codes in a costing system are used to collect data about costs and income and analyse these amounts into categories that the organisation finds useful. Sales and purchase invoices and other documents that contain data to be analysed will be 'coded' and the value amount together with the code will be entered into a computerised costing system or database.

We have learned about classifying costs:

- by element (materials, labour, expenses)
- by nature (direct and indirect)

cost centres and cost behaviour **31**

We have also learnt that cost centres, profit centres and investment centres can be used to identify sections of a business. A coding system can use these ways of classifying costs and classifying income.

For example, a clothing manufacturer might use a coding system where the first part of the code denotes the profit centre or cost centre, and the second part of the code (the sub-code) denotes a sub-classification based on whether the data is sales income, direct cost, or indirect cost.

If this code system was **alpha-numeric**, the amount of income from the **sales of dresses** could be coded to:

> B10   if B related to the profit centre 'dresses'
> and 10 was the sub-code for 'sales income'

The cost of machinists' **wages in the sewing section** could be coded to:

> H30   if H related to the cost centre 'sewing section'
> and 30 was the sub-code for 'direct cost'

Remember that the coding system will be designed to suit the needs of each individual organisation. The above example is quite a simple one, but demonstrates how a coding system could work.

We will now use a Case Study to illustrate in more detail how a coding system works.

CLASSY LIMITED: USING COSTING CODES

situation

Classy Limited is an educational company that runs courses for accountancy trainees and other office staff.

It uses a coding system for the elements of cost (materials, labour and expenses), with further classification into direct and indirect costs.

The coding used is as follows:

Element	Code	Nature	Code
Materials	100	Direct	X
		Indirect	Y
Labour	200	Direct	X
		Indirect	Y
Expenses	300	Direct	X
		Indirect	Y

required

Identify codes for the following costs:

- wages of tutor
- rent of classroom
- handouts and stationery for students' use
- power, light and heat in classroom
- wages of manager
- insurance of equipment

solution

• wages of tutor	200X
• rent of classroom	300Y
• handouts and stationery for students' use	100X
• power, light and heat in classroom	300Y
• wages of manager	200Y
• insurance of equipment	300Y

Note: for an example of an alternative coding system, see Activity 2.3 on page 45.

COST BEHAVIOUR

So far in this chapter we have seen how we can classify costs according to the main **elements** of materials, labour and expenses. We can classify the **nature** of costs as direct or indirect, and also according to their **function**. We can use cost centres to help with this analysis.

One further way that costs can be classified is based on the way that costs change when the level of output changes. This is known as **cost behaviour**.

what does 'cost behaviour' mean?

What we mean by **cost behaviour** is the way in which costs alter with **changes in the level of output or activity**. For example:

- for a **manufacturing** organisation, the **quantity of items** produced
- for a **service** organisation, the **volume of services** provided

When the output of an organisation changes, some costs will stay the same, while others will change. There are three main ways that costs may behave:

- **fixed** costs
- **variable** costs
- **semi-variable** costs

Remember that we are only interested here in the way that costs change because of changes in output or activity – not because of changes in price or any other reason unrelated to output or activity.

fixed costs

Fixed costs do not alter when the level of output or activity changes.

For example, the rent of a furniture factory will not change just because a different number of chairs were made in one month compared to the previous month. The factory rent is therefore said to behave as a **fixed cost**. This does not mean that the factory rent will never change – it means that it does not change because the output of the factory changes.

Suppose that the rent for a furniture factory was £5,000 per month. This total monthly rent would the same whether 100 chairs were made or 1,000 chairs were made. It would still be £5,000 per month if the factory shut down for a holiday and no chairs at all were made. If we drew a graph based on the total rent and the number of chairs made we would see that it produced a straight horizontal line, as follows:

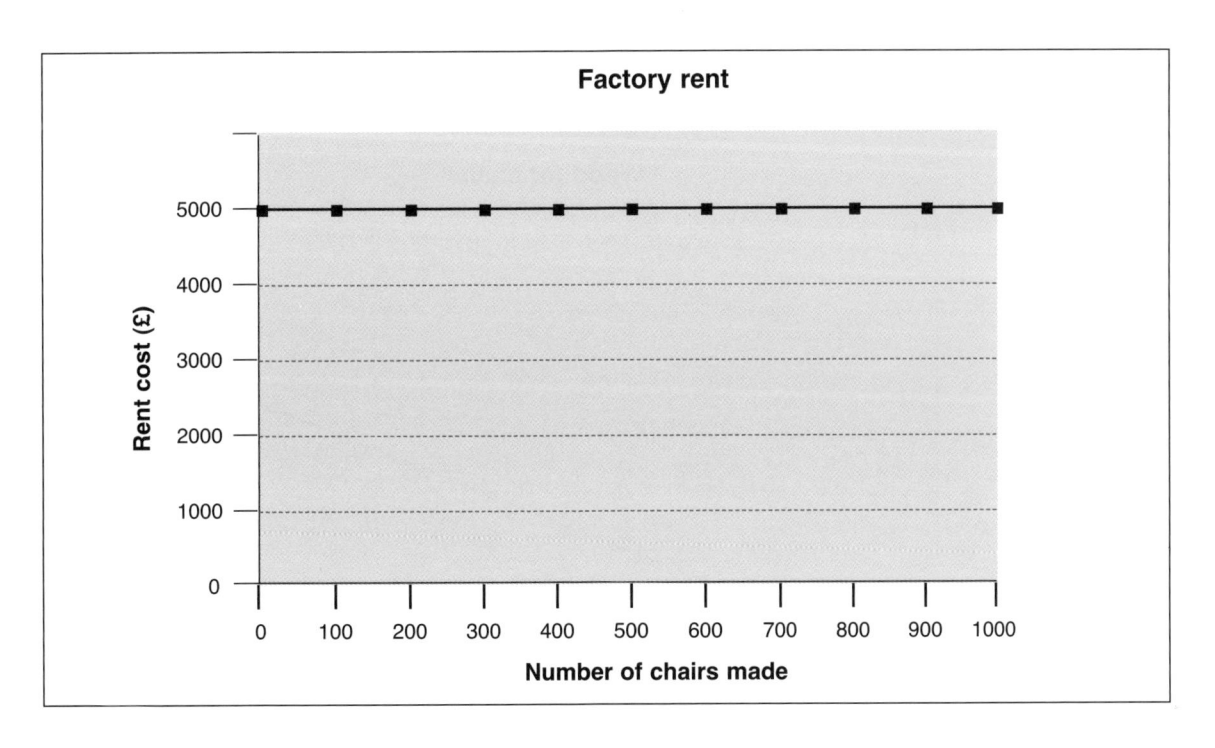

Factory rent

[Graph showing Rent cost (£) on y-axis from 0 to 5000, Number of chairs made on x-axis from 0 to 1000, with a horizontal line at £5000]

Notice that we are examining the total cost of rent (for a month) in this example, and can see that this does not change. If we were to calculate the cost of rent per chair made then we would see that the more chairs that were made, the lower the rent cost would be for each chair. This is a feature of fixed costs – the cost is fixed in total and this means that the greater the output the lower the cost per unit. Lower costs per unit are the result of spreading fixed costs over more units.

variable costs

Variable costs change in proportion to the level of output or activity.

For example, if the output doubles then the total of a variable cost would also double.

The total cost of wood for chairs that are made in a furniture factory will depend on the number of chairs that are made. If more chairs are made, the total cost of wood will be greater. We would expect the cost of wood to make 200 chairs to be twice as much as the cost of wood to make 100 chairs. This is because the wood for each chair will cost the same, and more chairs means more wood. We can ignore issues like quantity discounts when considering cost behaviour at this stage of our studies.

Suppose that the cost of wood for each chair is £20. That means that if 100 chairs are made the total cost of wood will be £20 x 100 = £2,000. If 200 chairs were made the total cost of wood would be £20 x 200 = £4,000, and so on. A graph of the total cost of wood would look like this:

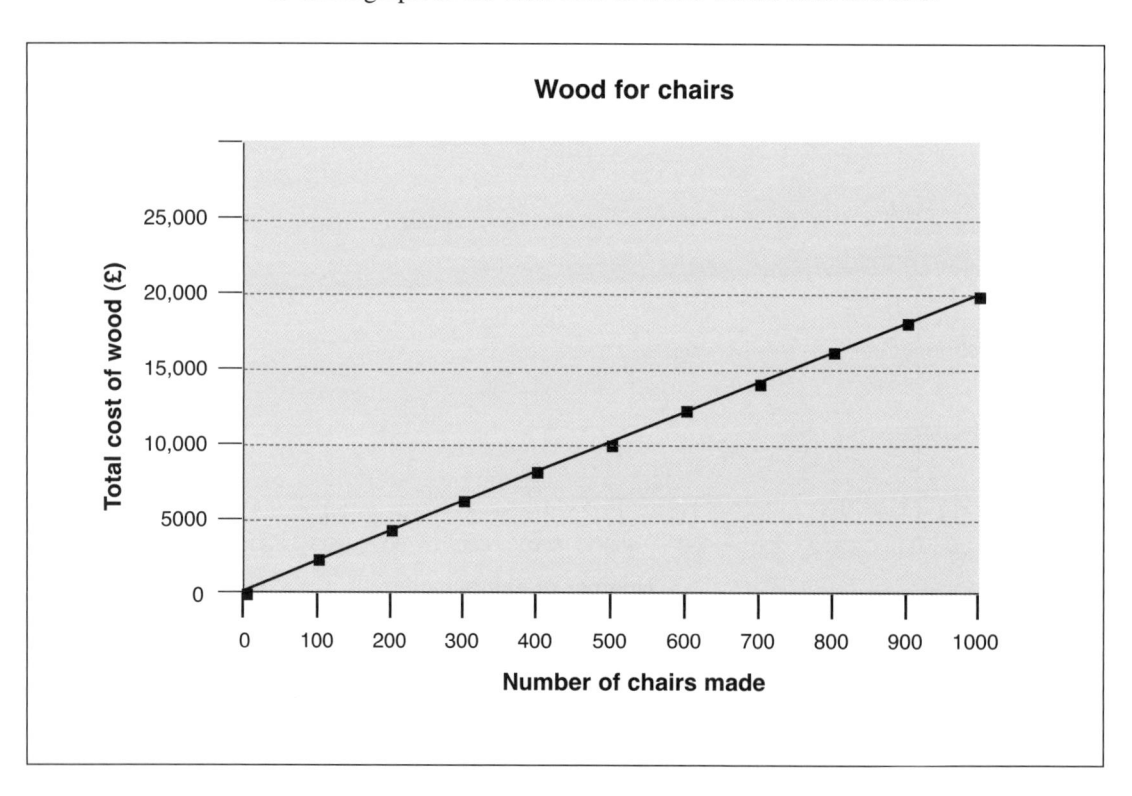

Wood for chairs

[Graph showing Total cost of wood (£) on y-axis from 0 to 25,000 plotted against Number of chairs made on x-axis from 0 to 1000, with a straight line rising from origin]

Total variable costs will always look like this on a graph. The cost line starts in the bottom left corner where there is zero output and zero cost. The points then form a straight line as the total cost rises in proportion to the output.

When the output increases variable costs per unit do not change. In our example the cost of wood per chair remained £20 regardless of the number of chairs made. Contrast this with fixed costs that stay the same in total, but reduce as a cost per item when the output rises.

semi-variable costs

Semi-variable costs contain both a fixed element and a variable element.

When output (or activity) changes, part of the cost will remain fixed, and part of the cost will change in proportion to the activity. This means that if output doubled a semi-variable cost would increase, but it would not double – the increase would be less than that because the fixed costs stay the same.

Suppose that in a furniture factory a person was employed as an assembler - to fit the parts of the chairs together. If the assembler was paid a basic salary of £1,000 per month, plus a bonus amount of £1 for every chair that he or she assembled then the cost of employing this person would be a semi-variable cost. The basic pay would not change no matter how many chairs were assembled – this part would represent a **fixed cost**. The bonus based on the number of chairs assembled would represent a **variable cost** as is would change in proportion to the number of chairs assembled. Together the total would be a **semi-variable cost**.

The **total cost** of employing the assembler for a month will look like this on a graph:

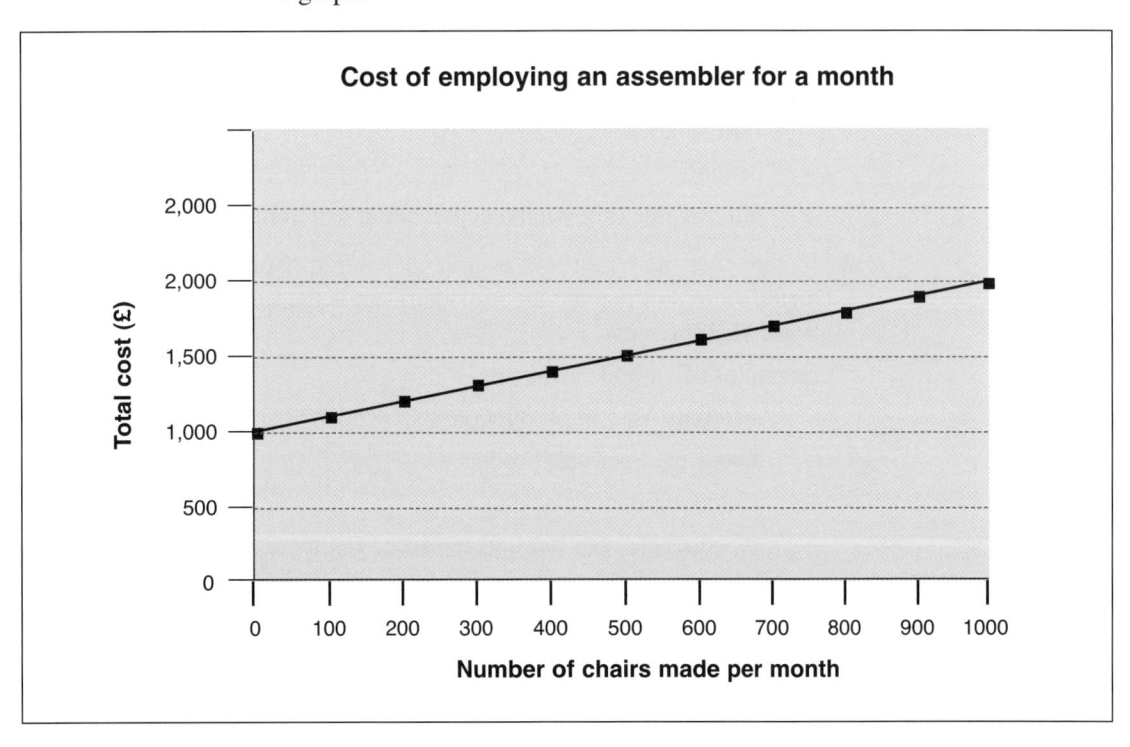

Cost of employing an assembler for a month

The total cost follows a straight line that starts on the far left at the axis where the only cost is the fixed cost. This is because when no chairs are made the assembler will be paid just the basic £1,000. The line then rises by £1 for each chair. In this example, the fixed element of the cost is £1,000 per month, and the variable element is £1 per chair. The graph is really like a fixed cost graph with a variable cost graph added on top of it.

Note that the total labour cost **per unit** for a semi-variable cost will reduce as the output increases.

IDENTIFYING COST BEHAVIOUR

As we saw in the last section the three main types of cost behaviour are costs that are fixed, variable and semi-variable. It is important that you can identify how a certain cost is likely to behave if you are provided with some basic information. This is easy to do if you understand the different relationships between cost and output and think the situation through.

The following points and examples may help with identification of cost behaviour.

- If the cost is based on a time period and the amount does not depend on output then it will be a **fixed cost**.

    Examples of fixed costs are:
    - rent and rates
    - insurance
    - staff salaries
    - heating
    - fall in value (known as 'depreciation') of vehicles

- If the cost is based on a unit of output (for example per item manufactured or per service provided) and is the same for each one, then it is a **variable cost**.

    Examples of variable costs are:
    - materials used in production
    - labour paid per unit produced
    - packaging materials
    - expenses charged per unit produced (eg royalties)
    - vehicle fuel for a delivery organisation

- If the cost is based on a combination of time period cost and per unit cost then it will behave as a **semi-variable cost**.

cost centres and cost behaviour 37

Examples of semi-variable costs are:
- labour paid on a weekly wage basis plus a production bonus
- power for production machinery if charged at a flat rate plus a charge based on amount used

We will now use two Case Studies, each based on a different type of organisation, to practise identifying the way that costs behave.

Case Study 1

JEAN'S JEANS: IDENTIFYING COST BEHAVIOUR

situation

You work in the costing section of Jean's Jeans, a company that makes clothing. You have been asked to identify how each of the costs shown below is likely to behave, as a preliminary part of a cost planning exercise.

Costs
- material for clothes
- factory rent
- power for sewing machines in factory (charged per unit of electricity)
- factory supervisors' wages (paid a flat rate plus a production-based bonus)
- packaging materials
- telephone (charged at a flat rate plus an amount per call; more calls are made when more clothes are being produced)
- office rates
- delivery drivers' pay (paid a flat rate plus a bonus per package delivered)
- factory heating

required

Complete the following table by inserting the costs into the most appropriate column.

Fixed Costs	Variable Costs	Semi-variable Costs
Factory rent	Material for clothes	Factory supervisors
Office rates	Power for sewing machines	Telephone
Factory heating	Packaging materials	Delivery drivers

solution

Fixed Costs	Variable Costs	Semi-variable Costs
Factory rent	Material for clothes	Factory supervisors' wages
Office rates	Power for sewing machines in factory	Telephone
Factory heating	Packaging materials	Delivery drivers' pay

Case Study 2

BLOWN AWAY: IDENTIFYING COST BEHAVIOUR

situation

You work for Blown Away, a company that provides hot air balloon rides. Each trip is for two passengers and a pilot, with a recovery vehicle following on the ground. You have been asked to identify how each of the costs shown below is likely to behave, as a preliminary part of a cost planning exercise.

Costs

- insurance (charged per year, regardless of number of flights)
- fuel for balloon
- pilot's pay (a basic amount plus a bonus per flight)
- car tax (vehicle excise duty) for recovery vehicle
- pay for recovery vehicle driver (paid per flight)
- refreshments for passengers after every flight
- advertising costs
- annual rent of take-off site
- fuel for recovery vehicle
- annual subscription to weather forecasting service
- use of mobile telephone for contact between pilot and recovery vehicle driver (paid at a flat rate plus a charge per call)

cost centres and cost behaviour 39

required

Complete the following table by inserting the costs into the most appropriate column.

Fixed Costs	Variable Costs	Semi-variable Costs
Insurance Car tax Advertising cost Rent Subscription	Fuel for balloon ~~Car tax~~ Pay for recovery Refreshment for passenger after every flight. Fuel for recovery vehicle	Pilot's pay Mobile phone

solution

Fixed Costs	Variable Costs	Semi-variable Costs
Insurance	Fuel for balloon	Pilots' pay
Car tax for recovery vehicle	Wages of recovery vehicle driver	Use of mobile telephone
Advertising costs	Refreshments for passengers	
Rent of take-off site	Fuel for recovery vehicle	
Subscription to weather forecasting service		

COST BEHAVIOUR CALCULATIONS

Now that we have studied cost behaviour and are able to identify fixed, variable, and semi-variable costs we can use this knowledge to carry out calculations.

Study the worked example on the next page.

worked example

If we know that variable costs of a product total £15 per unit, and that fixed costs are £1,000 per month, we can calculate the total costs for a given number of units.

- 100 units made in a month would result in costs of

Variable Costs	(£15 x 100)	£1,500
Fixed Costs		£1,000
Total Costs		£2,500

- 500 units made in a month would result in costs of

Variable Costs	(£15 x 500)	£7,500
Fixed Costs		£1,000
Total Costs		£8,500

We can also calculate the total cost per unit, (often known as the 'unit cost') by dividing the total costs by the number of units.

- If 100 units are made the cost per unit would be

    £2,500 ÷ 100 = £25.00 per unit

- If 500 units are made the cost per unit would be

    £8,500 ÷ 500 = £17.00 per unit

Notice that by making more units the unit cost is lower. This will always occur where part of the total cost behaves as a fixed cost, since there are more units to spread the fixed cost over.

If required, the unit cost could be analysed in various ways.

Suppose that in our example the variable cost of £15 per unit is made up of materials £10, and labour £5, and the fixed cost of £1,000 per month is overheads. We could then calculate the following costs, based on producing 500 units in a month.

	Total Cost	Unit Cost
Materials (£10 per unit)	£5,000	£10
Labour (£5 per unit)	£2,500	£5
Overheads (£1,000 per month)	£1,000	£2
Total	£8,500	£17

Notice in this table that the total cost figures are based on the same ones that we calculated earlier, and that the unit cost is the same in total as we previously calculated.

cost centres and cost behaviour 41

In summary:

- to calculate **total costs**:

    multiply variable costs per unit by the output, and add to the fixed costs

- to calculate **unit costs:**

    divide the fixed costs by the output, and add to the variable costs per unit

We will now use a Case Study to make sure that we can deal with similar calculations when they are presented in a slightly different way.

Case Study

BEHAVE!
COST BEHAVIOUR CALCULATIONS

situation

'Behave!' is a dog training service that provides hour-long sessions to help owners control their pets. A unit of output for this organisation is one session.

The following table contains accurate data based on one month, and needs to be completed for various activity levels.

Sessions	Fixed Costs £	Variable Costs £	Total Costs £	Unit Cost £
100	£2,000	£2,000	£4,000	£40
150	2,000	3,600	5,000	33
200	2,000	4,000	6,000	30
250	2,000	5,000	7,000	28

required

Complete the table, showing fixed costs, variable costs, total costs and unit cost at the different activity levels (numbers of sessions). Show all amounts to the nearest £.

solution

Sessions	Fixed Costs	Variable Costs	Total Costs	Unit Cost
100	£2,000	£2,000	£4,000	£40
150	£2,000	£3,000	£5,000	£33
200	£2,000	£4,000	£6,000	£30
250	£2,000	£5,000	£7,000	£28

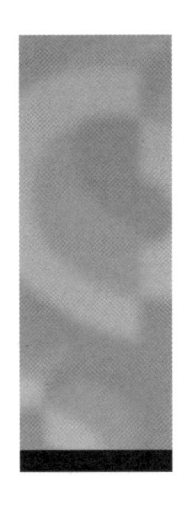

The calculations can be carried out as follows:

- the fixed costs remain at £2,000 for all activity levels, so that column can easily be completed

- the variable cost per unit can be calculated from the variable cost that is given, divided by the number of sessions, £2,000 ÷ 100 = £20; this can be used to calculate all the figures in the variable cost column by multiplying by the appropriate number of sessions (eg 150 sessions x £20 = £3,000).

- the total costs are calculated by adding the fixed and variable costs together.

- the unit cost is calculated by dividing the total cost by the appropriate number of sessions (eg £5,000 ÷ 150 = £33)

Chapter Summary

- Cost centres are used to help with the functional analysis of costs. Costs are collected in cost centres, and can be used to provide information to the manager responsible for the performance of a specific cost centre.

- Profit centres are used to collect data about both costs and income, and can therefore provide information about the profitability of that part of the organisation.

- Investment centres are used to collect data about income, costs and the amount invested. In this way profitability can be compared to the level of investment.

- Coding systems are used in many contexts and there are many examples of codes that we all use every day including postcodes and dialling codes. Different code structures have different advantages and disadvantages.

- Coding is used extensively for analysis of costs and income in costing systems. The types used mainly in costing are numeric, alphabetic and alpha-numeric. Codes may be used to analyse costs based on element, nature, cost centre or function or a combination of these classifications.

- Cost behaviour examines how costs respond to changes in the level of output or activity. Costs can behave in one of several ways, including as fixed costs, variable costs, and semi-variable costs.

- An understanding of cost behaviour can be used to enable the calculation of total costs and unit costs using simple arithmetic.

Key Terms

cost centre — a section of an organisation to which costs can be charged. The number and type of cost centre would depend on the requirements of the organisation

profit centre — a section of an organisation to which costs can be charged, income can be identified, and profits can be calculated

investment centre — a section of an organisation to which costs can be charged, income can be identified and investment can be measured

coding system — a way of using unique headings to analyse data. They can also be used to place the data in logical order if required

numeric code — a code made up entirely of numbers

alphabetic code — a code made up entirely of letters of the alphabet

alpha-numeric code — a code made up of a combination of numbers and letters

cost behaviour — the way that costs alter with changes in the level of output or activity

fixed cost — a cost that does not alter when the level of output or activity changes

variable cost — a cost that changes in proportion to the level of output or activity

semi-variable cost — a cost that contains both a fixed element and a variable element

Activities

2.1 Identify which one of the following lists could be used as cost centres for a company that manufactures windows.

(a) Materials; Labour; Overheads
(b) Frame Construction; Glazing; Administration; Distribution ✓
(c) Direct Costs; Indirect Costs
(d) Prime Cost; Manufacturing Overheads; Non-Production Overheads

Answer (a) or (b) or (c) or (d)

2.2 Cliff Beach Limited is a company that owns two shops in a seaside town. One shop is called Clifftop, and the other is called Beachside. Each shop is an investment centre. Administration for the shops is carried out in a separate cost centre.

The following is an extract from the coding manual used by the company.

Investment or Cost Centre	Code
Administration	A
Beachside Shop	B
Clifftop Shop	C

Revenue, Cost, or Investment	Code
Shop sales revenue	100
Shop purchases for resale	200
Labour costs	300
Overheads	400
Investment in shop assets	900

Each code consists of a letter followed by a 3 digit number.

Complete the following table with the appropriate codes.

Transaction	Code
Sales in Beachside shop	B100
Cost of paying wages of shop staff at Clifftop	C 300
Purchase of new display shelving for Beachside	B 900
Purchase of goods for resale at Clifftop shop	C 200
Cost of electricity at Clifftop shop	C 400
Cost of paying wages of company administrator	A 300

cost centres and cost behaviour 45

2.3 Roadways Limited is a transport company that provides a delivery service for its customers' goods.

It uses a coding system based on material, labour and overheads, with further classification into direct and indirect costs.

The coding used is as follows:

	Code	Nature	Code
Material	A	Direct	100
		Indirect	200
Labour	B	Direct	100
		Indirect	200
Overheads	C	Direct	100
		Indirect	200

Code the following costs, extracted from invoices and payroll, using the table below.

Cost	Code
• wages of drivers	B100
• loss in value (depreciation) of vehicles	C200
• fuel for vehicles	A100
• rent of premises	C200
• wages of maintenance staff	B200
• advanced driving courses	C200

2.4 Eagle Books, a publisher of textbooks and general books, uses a numerical coding structure. The business is split into four divisions: academic textbooks, novels, children's books and sports books – each division is a profit centre. There is also a cost centre for administration. Each profit/cost centre has a two-digit code; each income or cost has a three-digit code. Therefore each transaction is coded as xx/xxx.

An extract from the company's coding policy manual is as follows:

profit/cost centre code	profit/cost centre name
20	academic textbooks
30	novels
40	children's books
50	sports books
60	administration

analysis code	revenue or expense
110	printing
210	basic pay
220	overtime
230	holiday pay
310	authors' royalties
320	rates
330	heating and lighting
340	telephone
350	building maintenance
360	vehicle running costs
370	advertising
410	sales to bookshops
420	sales to wholesalers

From the coding policy manual extract given, you are to code the following income or cost transactions using the table below.

Transaction	Code
• Sales invoice showing the sale of £14,750 of academic textbooks to Orton Book Wholesalers Limited	20/420
• Printer's bill of £22,740 for printing sports books	50/110
• Payroll summary showing overtime of £840 last month in the children's book section	40/220
• Payment of £1,540 for advertising sports books in the magazine 'Sport Today'	50/370
• Telephone bill of £1,200 for the administration department	60/340
• Royalties of £88,245 paid to children's book authors	40/310
• Sales invoice showing the sale of £1,890 of novels to the Airport Bookshop	30/410

2.5 You work in the costing section of Doorcraft Ltd, a company that manufactures wooden doors. Each door is made by cutting up wood using a powered saw, and the wood pieces are screwed together. The door is then machine sanded and finally polished by hand.

An extract from the company's coding policy manual is as follows:

Each code is made up of three digits:

- the first digit shows the cost centre
- the second digit shows whether the cost is direct or indirect
- the third digit shows the element of cost (materials, labour, expenses)

Extract from cost centre list:

1　Factory – Wood cutting and door assembly
2　Factory – Door sanding and polishing
3　Office

Extract from list of analysis codes (second digit):

1　Direct
2　Indirect

Extract from list of analysis codes (third digit):

1　Material
2　Labour
3　Expenses

From the coding policy manual extract given you are to code the following expense transactions, using the table below.

Transaction	Code
• Wages of the carpenter who assembles the doors	1 1 2
• Sandpaper	2 1 1
• Saw sharpening service	1 2 3
• Wages of the cleaner who works in the door sanding and polishing section	2 2 2
• Office telephone costs	3 2 3
• Wood for manufacturing doors	1 1 1
• Wages of office worker	3 2 2

48 introduction to costing tutorial

2.6 Identify the following statements as either true or false by putting a tick in the relevant column of the table below.

	True	False
• Variable costs always include a time period cost		✓
• Fixed costs are based on a time period and the amount does not depend on output	✓	
• Semi-variable costs change directly with changes in the level of activity		✓

2.7 Identify the following statements as either true or false by putting a tick in the relevant column of the table below.

	True	False
• A variable cost is based on a unit of output and is the same for each one	✓	
• A fixed cost changes with changes in the level of activity		✓
• A semi-variable cost is based on a combination of a time period cost and a per unit cost	✓	

2.8 Classify the following costs as either fixed or variable by putting a tick in the relevant column of the table below.

Costs	Fixed	Variable
• Rent of premises	✓	
• Labour paid per unit produced		✓
• Staff salaries	✓	
• Packaging materials for goods produced		✓

2.9 Classify the following costs as either fixed or variable by putting a tick in the relevant column of the table below.

Costs	Fixed	Variable
• Insurance of vehicles	✓	
• Heating and lighting	✓	
• Materials used in production		✓
• Bonus paid to production workers for each extra unit of output		✓

2.10 You work in the costing section of Doorcraft Ltd, a company that manufactures wooden doors. Each door is made by cutting up wood using a powered saw, and the wood pieces are screwed together. The door is then machine sanded and finally polished by hand.

Classify the following costs incurred by their behaviour (fixed, variable or semi-variable) by putting a tick in the relevant column of the table below.

Costs	Fixed	Variable	Semi-variable
• Factory rates	✓		
• Power for saw and sanders in factory (charged per unit of electricity)		✓	
• Factory supervisors' wages (paid a time rate plus a production-based bonus)			✓
• Wood used in the production process		✓	
• Telephone (charged at a flat rate plus an amount per call)			✓
• Office rent	✓		
• Polish for finishing doors		✓	
• Delivery drivers' pay (paid a time rate plus a bonus per door delivered)			✓
• Factory lighting	✓		
• Wages of production staff who are paid according to the number of doors they make		✓	
• Salary of marketing manager	✓		

2.11 The following table contains data based on a company that makes a single product, and needs to be completed for different levels of production.

Output (units)	Fixed Costs	Variable Costs	Total Costs	Unit Cost
1,000	£30,000	£20,000	£50,000	£50
1,500	£ 30,000	£ 30,000	£ 60,000	£ 40
2,000	£ 30,000	£ 40,000	£ 70,000	£ 35
3,000	£ 30,000	£ 50,000	£ 80,000	£ 30

You are to complete the table, showing fixed costs, variable costs, total costs and unit cost for the different levels of production.

2.12 Complete the table below showing fixed costs, variable costs, total costs and unit cost for the different levels of production.

Output (units)	Fixed Costs	Variable Costs	Total Costs	Unit Cost
2,000	£12,000	£4,000	£16,000	£8
3,000	£ 12,000	£ 6,000	£ 18,000	£ 6
4,000	£ 12,000	£ 8,000	£ 20,000	£ 5
6,000	£ 12,000	£ 10,000	£ 22,000	£ 4

2.13 Complete the table below showing fixed costs, variable costs, total costs and unit cost for the different levels of production.

Output (units)	Fixed Costs	Variable Costs	Total Costs	Unit Cost
500	£8,000	£2,000	£10,000	£20
1,000	£ 8,000	£ 4,000	£ 12,000	£ 12
2,000	£ 8,000	£ 8,000	£ 16,000	£ 8
4,000	£ 8,000	£ 16,000	£ 24,000	£ 6

2.14 Victoria Ltd is costing a single product which has the following cost details:

Variable costs per unit

Material	£5
Labour	£4
Total fixed costs	£50,000

Complete the following total cost and unit cost table for a production level of 25,000 units.

	Total cost	Unit cost
Material	25,000 × 5 £ 125,000	£ 5
Labour	25,000 × 4 £ 100,000	£ 4
Overheads	£ 50,000	£ 2
Total	£ 275,000	£ 11 ~~,000~~

2.15 Albert Ltd is costing a single product which has the following cost details:

Variable costs per unit

Material	£10
Labour	£8
Total fixed costs	£90,000

Complete the following total cost and unit cost table for a production level of 30,000 units.

	Total cost	Unit cost
Material	30,000 × 10 £ 300,000	£ 10
Labour	30,000 × 8 £ 240,000	£ 8
Overheads	£ 90,000	£ 3
Total	£ 630,000	£ 21

3 Inventory valuation and the manufacturing account

this chapter covers...

In this chapter we will explain inventory (also called 'stock') held by an organisation – how it is classified, valued, and used to help calculate important costing information.

We will start by looking at inventory held by a manufacturing organisation and how it can be classified as it passes through the production process as:

- raw materials
- part-finished goods (work-in-progress)
- finished goods

We will then go on to describe the valuation methods that can be used by an organisation. As cost prices vary from time-to-time organisations need to establish a policy of how goods which may have been bought at different times are to be valued.

The three methods of inventory valuation which we will examine and use are:

- 'first in first out' (FIFO)
- 'last in first out' (LIFO), and
- 'weighted average cost' (AVCO).

We will describe how these methods work, and how they can be used to value inventory.

The final section of this chapter deals with the preparation of a manufacturing account which is a cost statement that shows the build up of costs, using valuations of raw materials, work-in-progress and finished goods.

TYPES OF INVENTORY

Inventory (also called 'stock') is held by a range of businesses.

- **trading organisations**, such as shops, that simply buy and then sell the same items – this is their 'inventory'
- **manufacturers** – businesses that manufacture products will hold inventory in various forms:
    - **raw materials** – these are the materials that have been bought by a manufacturing business and are ready to be transferred to the production area where they will be used to make the finished goods
    - **work-in-progress** – this comprises **part-finished products** that are awaiting completion
    - **finished goods** – as the name suggests, these are manufactured items that have been completed and are ready for sale

In your studies you may be asked to classify inventory held by manufacturing businesses into the above three categories based on their descriptions, as in the following Case Study.

Case Study

TYPES OF INVENTORY

situation

Each item in the following table needs to be classified into one of the following three categories: raw materials or work-in-progress or finished goods.

Inventory item and organisation	Classification
Flour held by a pizza manufacturer	
Onions held by a pizza manufacturer	
New cars held by a car manufacturer	
Sheet steel held by a car manufacturer	
Car bodies manufactured by a car manufacturer awaiting completion	
Pizza bases (without toppings) held by a pizza manufacturer	
Pizzas held by a pizza manufacturer	

The answer is on the next page.

solution

Inventory item and organisation	Classification
Flour held by a pizza manufacturer	raw materials
Onions held by a pizza manufacturer	raw materials
New cars held by a car manufacturer	finished goods
Sheet steel held by a car manufacturer	raw materials
Car bodies manufactured by a car manufacturer awaiting completion	work-in-progress
Pizza bases (without toppings) held by a pizza manufacturer	work-in-progress
Pizzas held by a pizza manufacturer	finished goods

INVENTORY VALUATION

the need for valuation

It is important to know how inventory can be valued because the valuation is used in the calculation of:

- the cost of items that have been used in the production process to make a finished product
- the cost of items that remain

These costs will eventually be needed, in the case of a business, in the calculation of profit. In this chapter we will describe the different ways in which raw materials can be valued in the **manufacturing** process.

The process that we will be considering is split into three stages:

1. raw materials for the manufacturing process are bought from a supplier at a quoted purchase price
2. these materials are then stored on the premises (in a store area or warehouse) until needed for production
3. the goods are transferred to the production process when required

This process is illustrated in the diagram at the top of the next page.

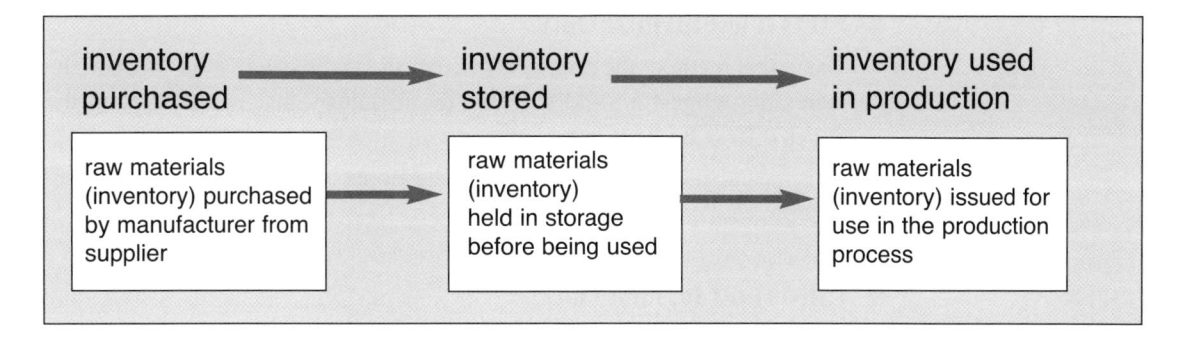

inventory valuation and the manufacturing account   55

```
inventory          →    inventory         →    inventory used
purchased               stored                 in production

raw materials           raw materials          raw materials
(inventory) purchased   (inventory)            (inventory) issued for
by manufacturer from    held in storage        use in the production
supplier                before being used      process
```

We are mainly concerned with the middle part of this diagram – the 'stores' section of the business. We need to know how materials that have been purchased can be valued.

the problem with valuation

If buying prices are always the same every time raw materials are bought then the same purchase price could be used for valuations and life would be simple.

The problem arises because **purchase prices change from time to time**, so inventory held in the stores may well be bought in at different prices, which makes valuation of that inventory difficult.

Is the valuation based on the most recent price paid? Or the price of the oldest inventory in the stores? Or even an average price of all the different prices paid for the same type of inventory?

In the next section we will describe three commonly used different methods of inventory valuation.

VALUATION METHODS

There are three main methods of valuing inventory. These are normally known by their abbreviations:

- FIFO (first in, first out)
- LIFO (last in, first out)
- AVCO (average cost)

We will explain and illustrate these on the pages that follow.

- **FIFO (First In, First Out)**

    Using this method, the purchase price of the inventory that has been in the stores the longest is used to value the inventory that is issued from the stores – **first in, first out**.

    This means that the inventory left in the stores is valued at the most recent cost prices.

- **LIFO (Last In, First Out)**

    The principle used is quite different from FIFO because the valuation of the inventory issued is based on the cost of the inventory most recently purchased – **last in first out**.

    This means that the inventory left in the stores is valued at the older cost prices.

- **AVCO (Average Cost)**

    In this method, an overall **average cost** (or **average weighted cost**) is calculated for the inventory held in the stores, using the formula:

    $$\text{average cost} = \frac{\text{total cost of goods in stores}}{\text{number of items in stores}}$$

    This average cost is then used to value the inventory issued from the stores. This also means that a new average cost must be calculated each time that a new purchase of inventory is made.

We will now illustrate FIFO, LIFO and AVCO with a numerical example to explain how each system works. Then in the section that follows we will describe the characteristics and features of the three valuation methods.

We will take as an example a manufacturing business which buys in raw materials, stores the raw materials and then releases the raw materials to the manufacturing process.

The raw materials (inventory) in this illustration are in 'units'. In reality they could be kilos of chemicals, metres of cloth, litres of oil – or whatever raw materials the business in question uses to make its product.

The table at the top of the next page shows the quantities of units as they are purchased, stored and released for production:

- **Receipts**: here there are two purchases of inventory
- **Issues**: there is one issue of inventory
- **Balance**: this shows the number of units of inventory left in the stores after each transaction (in reality there would be an 'opening balance' but this is omitted here for the sake of simplicity)

inventory valuation and the manufacturing account **57**

Receipts	Issues	Balance
Quantity	Quantity	Quantity
100		100
150		250
	80	170

You can see from this table that it works on the basis of a running account with the balance in the right hand column. The figures involved are:

- Purchases: 100 units + 150 units = 250 units in the store
- Issues: 250 units – 80 units = 170 units left in the store

We will now expand this table to include money amounts so that we can work out the value of inventory, using the three methods of FIFO, LIFO and AVCO. The purchases made were: 100 units @ £40 per unit and 150 units @ £35 per unit.

FIFO (First In, First Out)

Using FIFO we assume that the inventory was issued in the order that it was bought. This would value the inventory issued to production at £40 per unit, and value the inventory still in stock partly at £40 per unit and partly at £35 per unit. The following table shows the values as well as quantities in all three columns.

FIFO

Receipts			Issues			Balance	
Quantity	Cost per unit	Total cost	Quantity	Value per unit	Total value	Quantity	Total value
100	£40	£4,000				100	£4,000
150	£35	£5,250				250	£9,250
			80	£40	£3,200	170	£6,050

This method values the issues in this example at £40 per unit x 80 units = £3,200.

That leaves the balance held with a value of £9,250 – £3,200 = £6,050.

This value is equal to the inventory remaining from each purchase:

From the first purchase	(100 – 80) =	20 units x £40	=	£800
From the second purchase		150 units x £35	=	£5,250
Total				£6,050

LIFO (Last In, First Out)

LIFO is different from FIFO because the valuation of the inventory issued is based on the cost of the inventory most **recently** purchased and not the oldest purchase.

This method would value the inventory issued to production at £35 per unit and value the inventory still in stock partly at £40 per unit and partly at £35 per unit, although in different proportions to the last method. The following table shows how these values would appear.

LIFO

\multicolumn{3}{c}{Receipts}			\multicolumn{3}{c}{Issues}			\multicolumn{2}{c}{Balance}
Quantity	Cost per unit	Total cost	Quantity	Value per unit	Total value	Quantity	Total value
100	£40	£4,000				100	£4,000
150	£35	£5,250				250	£9,250
			80	£35	£2,800	170	£6,450

This method values the issues in this example at £35 per unit x 80 units = £2,800

That leaves the balance held with a value of £9,250 - £2,800 = £6,450.

This value is equal to the inventory remaining from each purchase:

From the first purchase:	100 units x £40	=	£4,000
From the second purchase: (150 – 80) =	70 units x £35	=	£2,450
Total			£6,450

AVCO (Average Cost)

As we have already seen, when using the AVCO method of valuation, an overall average cost is calculated for the inventory held in the stores, using the formula:

$$\text{average cost} = \frac{\text{total cost of goods in stores}}{\text{number of items in stores}}$$

In the example we are using, we will work out the average cost of the inventory when it was purchased, and then use that average cost for both the next issue (80 units) and also the balance of inventory remaining (170 units).

The average value per unit is calculated as £9,250 ÷ 250 units = £37 per unit (see the table below).

AVCO

Receipts			Issues			Balance	
Quantity	Cost per unit	Total cost	Quantity	Value per unit	Total value	Quantity	Total value
100	£40	£4,000				100	£4,000
150	£35	£5,250				250	£9,250
			80	£37	£2,960	170	£6,290

AVCO values the issues in this example at £37 per unit x 80 units = £2,960.

That leaves the balance held in the stores with a value of £9,250 – £2,960 = £6,290.

This value is equal to 170 units x £37 = £6,290.

inventory valuations – summary

Each method of valuation will give a different answer, but each method is equally valid. In the example given we probably would not know which delivery of inventory was actually used for the issue, but that does not matter. The three inventory valuations methods are based on making assumptions about the way that inventory is used up, but these assumptions are only for valuation purposes – it is not relevant if the goods are actually used in that order or not.

CHARACTERISTICS OF INVENTORY VALUATION METHODS

The table on the next page summarises the key characteristics of the three methods of inventory valuation that we have examined.

CHARACTERISTICS OF INVENTORY VALUATION METHODS

	FIFO	LIFO	AVCO
VALUATION OF ISSUES			
Issues of inventory are valued at the oldest purchase prices	✓		
Issues of inventory are valued at the most recent purchase prices		✓	
Issues of inventory are valued at the weighted average cost of purchases			✓
VALUATION OF INVENTORY BALANCE			
Inventory is valued at the most recent purchase costs	✓		
Inventory is valued at the oldest purchase costs		✓	
Inventory is valued at the weighted average cost of purchases			✓

This table, together with what you have learned earlier about FIFO, LIFO and AVCO, will enable you to answer true or false statements which may be asked in assessments. Try the following statements by putting a tick in the relevant column of the table (answers are at the bottom of the page):

		True	False
1.	FIFO costs issues of inventory in the opposite order to which it was received		✓
2.	AVCO costs issues of inventory in the same order to which it was received		✓
3.	LIFO costs issues of inventory at the latest purchase prices	✓	
4.	LIFO values closing inventory at the oldest purchase prices	✓	
5.	FIFO values closing inventory at the most recent purchase costs	✓	
6.	AVCO values closing inventory at the weighted average cost of purchases	✓	

choosing an inventory valuation method

A business will need to decide which method of inventory valuation it will use. Although the examples we have used show the effect of using each method of inventory valuation, a business would make a decision as to which method is most appropriate for its needs, and then use it consistently.

Answers: 1. False; 2. False; 3. True; 4. True; 5. True; 6. True

CALCULATION OF INVENTORY VALUATIONS

In the examples of inventory valuation on pages 57-59 we used two purchases and one issue to illustrate each of the three methods. In the Case Study which follows on the next page we will present a practical example of these calculations.

This time we will provide an opening balance of inventory held, which adds another step to the calculation process. The principle is exactly the same as the presentation of any running balance account, such as shown in a bank statement: you start with a balance, enter 'in' and 'out' transactions and finish with a balance.

The key to accurate valuation calculations is to work through the figures from the earliest transaction to the latest, carrying out the required valuations of issues and balances in strict date order. This means that:

- where there is a starting balance and valuation, it is used in conjunction with the next purchase or issue to calculate the next balance and its valuation
- where purchases are made, the new balance is calculated and valued using the previous balance and adding in the quantity and value of the purchase
- where issues are made, the quantity is deducted from the previous inventory balance, and the issue valuation is deducted from the previous inventory valuation

Using this logical approach you will find that the arithmetic works for both **quantities** and **values:**

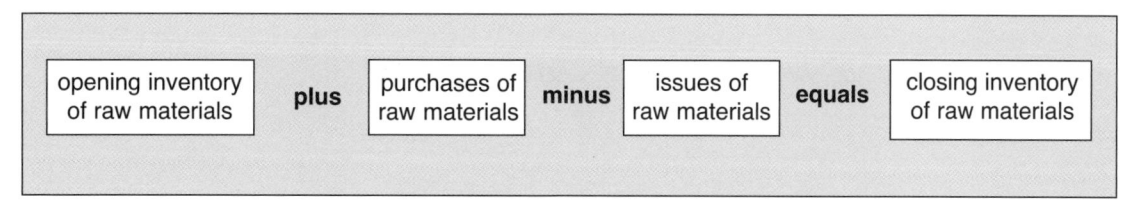

| opening inventory of raw materials | **plus** | purchases of raw materials | **minus** | issues of raw materials | **equals** | closing inventory of raw materials |

This is a useful check that your calculations make sense.

It is also important to use clear and accurate workings, so that you can easily see which values apply to which quantities. These workings could be inserted into a table (as is carried out in the next case study) or placed elsewhere if there is no room.

Case Study

FUEL STOP: INVENTORY VALUATION METHODS

situation

The Fuel Stop is a garage that buys fuel in bulk, and sells it to passing motorists. The fuel is held in a large tank, and deliveries are arranged so that the tank does not run dry. The following table shows a summary of the order of movements in fuel inventory during one week in litres.

Receipts (Purchases)			Issues (Sales)			Balance		
Quantity	Cost per litre	Total cost	Quantity	Value per litre	Total value	Quantity	Value per litre	Total value
						2,000	£0.90	£1,800
10,000	£1.20	£12,000						
			8,000					

required

Set up three tables to calculate valuations of issues, and quantities and valuations of all balances, using:

(a) FIFO (First in first out) valuation

(b) LIFO (Last in first out) valuation

(c) AVCO (Average cost) valuation

solution - FIFO

The table appears as follows:

Receipts (Purchases)			Issues (Sales)			Balance		
Quantity	Cost per litre	Total cost	Quantity	Value per litre	Total value	Quantity	Value per litre	Total value
						2,000	£0.90	£1,800
10,000	£1.20	£12,000				2,000 10,000 12,000	£0.90 £1.20	£1,800 £12,000 £13,800
			2,000 6,000 8,000	£0.90 £1.20	£1,800 £7,200 £9,000	4,000	£1.20	£4,800

Study the order and workings for the calculations in this solution. The following is a summary of what has taken place:

- Note that there is an opening balance of 2,000 litres, valued at £1,800 (90p per litre).

- The receipt of 10,000 litres at £1.20 is added to the opening balance, but the make-up of the value of the new balance is clearly shown so that the earliest part can be used first for the next issue.

- The issue of 8,000 litres is split into 2,000 litres and 6,000 litres to agree with the order of arrival of the petrol within the previous balance. This logic is continued in the calculation of the new balance, and we can see that all the litres at £0.90 have gone, and only 4,000 litres are left at £1.20 per litre, which represents the remaining part of the last receipt.

The arithmetic for both quantities and values is as follows:

	Quantities (litres)	Values (£)
Opening inventory balance	2,000	£1,800
+ Purchases	10,000	£12,000
- Issues	(8,000)	(£9,000)
= Closing inventory balance	4,000	£4,800

solution - LIFO

The table appears as follows:

Receipts (Purchases)			Issues (Sales)			Balance		
Quantity	Cost per litre	Total cost	Quantity	Value per litre	Total value	Quantity	Value per litre	Total value
						2,000	£0.90	£1,800
10,000	£1.20	£12,000				2,000 10,000 12,000	£0.90 £1.20	£1,800 £12,000 £13,800
			8,000	£1.20	£9,600	2,000 2,000 4,000	£0.90 £1.20	£1,800 £2,400 £4,200

- Note that there is an opening balance of 2,000 litres, valued at £1,800 (90p per litre).
- The issue of 8,000 litres is not split, since the whole amount is matched against the most recent purchase of 10,000 litres. This leaves a balance which is split into 2,000 litres at £0.90 and 2,000 litres at £1.20.

The arithmetic for both quantities and values is as follows:

	Quantities (litres)	Values (£)
Opening inventory balance	2,000	£1,800
+ Purchases	10,000	£12,000
- Issues	(8,000)	(£9,600)
= Closing inventory balance	4,000	£4,200

solution - AVCO

The table appears as follows:

Receipts (Purchases)			Issues (Sales)			Balance		
Quantity	Cost per litre	Total cost	Quantity	Value per litre	Total value	Quantity	Value per litre	Total value
						2,000	£0.90	£1,800
10,000	£1.20	£12,000				2,000 10,000 12,000	£1.15	£1,800 £12,000 £13,800
			8,000	£1.15	£9,200	4,000	£1.15	£4,600

The AVCO valuation method requires a slightly different technique to the other two.

There is no need to keep track of each purchase, since each time more goods are received a new average cost is calculated. This average is used for issues and balances until more goods are purchased.

These are the calculation methods used:

- When the purchase is made, an average cost is calculated by adding separately the quantities and values, and then dividing the total value by the total quantity to arrive at an average value per litre.

  In this example the calculation is £13,800 ÷ 12,000 litres = £1.15 per litre.

- The £1.15 per litre is then used to value the next issue and also the remaining balance.

The overall calculation is as follows:

	Quantities (litres)	Values (£)
Opening inventory balance	2,000	£1,800
+ Purchases	10,000	£12,000
– Issues	(8,000)	(£9,200)
= Closing inventory balance	4,000	£4,600

USING INVENTORY VALUATIONS

So far in this chapter we have learned how to identify the different types of inventory. For a manufacturing business these are raw materials, work-in-progress (part-finished goods), and finished goods. The inventory valuations for these are used in the calculation of summary figures needed by a manufacturing business.

The summary figures of a manufacturing business are:

- direct materials used
- direct cost
- manufacturing cost
- cost of goods manufactured
- cost of goods sold

These are calculated for a period of time (for example a week, month or year), through the use of a cost statement called a 'manufacturing account'. We will now look in detail at what each summary figure means, and how it is calculated, and then put the information together in the manufacturing account format.

direct materials used

The term **direct materials** is one that we have used earlier in this book, and describes materials that can be identified directly with the units of output. We are going to consider a manufacturing business where the direct materials are all raw materials.

When we examined valuation methods, we noticed that raw materials are not always used immediately in manufacture, but are often stored for a time as inventory. The total figure that we need to calculate as direct materials used is equivalent to the valuation of issues from stores to production. The easiest way to calculate the amount of direct materials used is to follow the formula seen earlier (page 61) for raw materials:

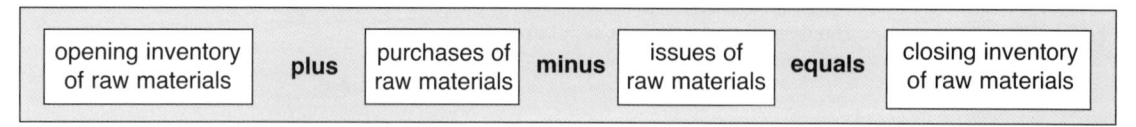

| opening inventory of raw materials | **plus** | purchases of raw materials | **minus** | issues of raw materials | **equals** | closing inventory of raw materials |

This is the same as:

| issues of raw materials | **equals** | opening inventory of raw materials | **plus** | purchases of raw materials | **minus** | closing inventory of raw materials |

In other words, the amount of raw materials used in production is made up of the amount of inventory at the beginning of the period, plus the amount purchased, less the amount that forms the closing inventory.

We therefore have a straightforward way to calculate the value of the direct materials used. The calculation forms the first part of the manufacturing account format and appears as follows. Sample figures have been inserted to illustrate the calculation.

Opening inventory of raw materials	£20,000
Purchases of raw materials	+ £40,000
Closing inventory of raw materials	– £15,000
DIRECT MATERIALS USED	= £45,000

It is important to note that the closing inventory valuation is always deducted in the calculation. (The symbols for '+', '–' and '=' are given in these examples to guide you, although they may not be given in assessments and activities.)

direct cost

This is the total of all direct costs (costs that can be directly identified with units of output). You will recall that the elements of cost are materials, labour and expenses. Since direct expenses are not very common, we are going to assume in our manufacturing account that direct cost consists only of direct materials used, plus direct labour. We can therefore build on our earlier manufacturing account format as follows, again using sample figures.

Opening inventory of raw materials	£20,000
Purchases of raw materials	+ £40,000
Closing inventory of raw materials	− £15,000
DIRECT MATERIALS USED	= £45,000
Direct labour	+ £35,000
DIRECT COST	= £80,000

manufacturing cost

The manufacturing cost of a product is made up of its direct cost and the manufacturing overheads associated with making that product.

After adding manufacturing overheads, the manufacturing cost statement comprises direct materials used, direct labour and manufacturing overheads. We then sub-total these to give a figure that may be called manufacturing cost. However, in order to calculate the cost of goods manufactured we first need to adjust for the inventory valuation of work-in-progress.

cost of goods manufactured

Cost of goods manufactured means the total costs of running the factory. It is calculated from direct cost by:

- adding the manufacturing overheads, which are the indirect costs of running the factory
- adjusting for work-in-progress at the beginning and end of the accounting period

Work-in-progress is any part-completed goods that may be in the factory at the beginning and at the end of the accounting period. For example, at any one time a car manufacturer will have partly-assembled cars going down the production line. It is the valuation of such partly-completed goods that gives the figure for work-in-progress – both at the beginning and at the end of the accounting period.

The adjustment for work-in-progress is made after the sub-total figure for manufacturing cost and we must:

- add opening inventory of work-in-progress
- deduct closing inventory of work-in-progress

To summarise this part of the manufacturing account, starting with the figure for direct cost:

- add manufacturing overheads
- sub-total for manufacturing cost
- add opening inventory of work-in-progress
- deduct closing inventory of work-in-progress
- sub-total for cost of goods manufactured

We can therefore see how the information using sample figures is building up in our manufacturing account format:

Opening inventory of raw materials	£20,000
Purchases of raw materials	+ £40,000
Closing inventory of raw materials	− £15,000
DIRECT MATERIALS USED	= £45,000
Direct labour	+ £35,000
DIRECT COST	= £80,000
Manufacturing overheads	+ £18,000
MANUFACTURING COST	= £98,000
Opening inventory of work-in-progress	+ £11,000
Closing inventory of work-in-progress	− £14,000
COST OF GOODS MANUFACTURED	= £95,000

Note that the closing inventory of work-in-progress is a deduction, in the same way that the closing inventory of raw materials is a deduction.

cost of goods sold

This is the final summary total, and it may be used in the calculation of profit by comparing it with the sales revenue. Cost of goods sold (also known as the cost of sales) must take account of the third category of inventory – finished goods. Cost of goods sold is made up of the value of the finished goods that existed at the start of the period, plus the cost of goods manufactured, but excluding the value of the finished goods inventory that remains at the end of the period. We therefore adjust the earlier total of factory cost of goods manufactured and:

- add opening inventory of finished goods
- deduct closing inventory of finished goods

The complete statement of a manufacturing account format now appears as follows, using the earlier sample figures, plus those for finished goods inventories:

Opening inventory of raw materials	£20,000
Purchases of raw materials	+ £40,000
Closing inventory of raw materials	– £15,000
DIRECT MATERIALS USED	= £45,000
Direct labour	+ £35,000
DIRECT COST	= £80,000
Manufacturing overheads	+ £18,000
MANUFACTURING COST	= £98,000
Opening inventory of work-in-progress	+ £11,000
Closing inventory of work-in-progress	– £14,000
COST OF GOODS MANUFACTURED	= £95,000
Opening inventory of finished goods	+ £17,000
Closing inventory of finished goods	– £16,000
COST OF GOODS SOLD	= £96,000

As noted earlier the symbols for '+', '–' and '=' are given to guide you, although they may not be given in assessments and activities.

We will now use a Case Study to practise preparing the manufacturing account format.

MAKEM LIMITED: MANUFACTURING ACCOUNT FORMAT

situation

You are employed by Makem Limited, a manufacturing company. A trainee has produced a list of data that needs to be assembled into a manufacturing account format. All the data has been checked for accuracy.

You are to reorder the following costs into a manufacturing account format for the year ended 31 December 20-1. Make sure that the arithmetic of your manufacturing account format is accurate.

DIRECT COST	£74,000
Opening inventory of raw materials	£12,000
Direct labour	£39,000
Closing inventory of finished goods	£15,000
COST OF GOODS SOLD	£98,000
Purchases of raw materials	£37,000
Opening inventory of finished goods	£19,000
MANUFACTURING COST	£97,000
Closing inventory of work-in-progress	£13,000
Opening inventory of work-in-progress	£10,000
Closing inventory of raw materials	£14,000
DIRECT MATERIALS USED	£35,000
Manufacturing overheads	£23,000
COST OF GOODS MANUFACTURED	£94,000

solution

Manufacturing account format for the year ended 31 December 20-1	
Opening inventory of raw materials	£12,000
Purchases of raw materials	£37,000
Closing inventory of raw materials	£14,000
DIRECT MATERIALS USED	£35,000
Direct labour	£39,000
DIRECT COST	£74,000
Manufacturing overheads	£23,000
MANUFACTURING COST	£97,000
Opening inventory of work-in-progress	£10,000
Closing inventory of work-in-progress	£13,000
COST OF GOODS MANUFACTURED	£94,000
Opening inventory of finished goods	£19,000
Closing inventory of finished goods	£15,000
COST OF GOODS SOLD	£98,000

Note that the symbols for '+', '–' and '=' have not been shown. For practice you may like to show them before checking the accuracy of the arithmetic.

Chapter Summary

- Inventories are held by manufacturing businesses in various forms – raw materials, work-in-progress and finished goods.

- A decision needs to be made on the method of inventory valuation that is to be used for raw materials. This is because inventory is made up of items bought at different prices and an assumption needs to be made for valuation purposes about the order that they are used up.

- The three main methods of inventory valuation for raw materials are:
    - first in first out (FIFO)
    - last in first out (LIFO)
    - average cost (AVCO)

  Each method involves calculating the value of issues and the remaining balance in different ways.

- Manufacturing accounts are used by businesses that produce goods to summarise the cost data for a period of time. The accounts are prepared in an established format and provide valuable information about the total costs at various stages. Manufacturing accounts use inventory valuations for raw materials, work-in-progress and finished goods at appropriate points to ensure that the information produced is valid and useful.

Key Terms

raw materials — the materials bought by manufacturing organisations and used to manufacture the finished products

work-in-progress — the name given to partly-completed items in a manufacturing organisation

finished goods — the items that have been manufactured and are ready for sale

first in first out (FIFO) — a method of inventory valuation that assumes that goods will be used up in the order that they are acquired (for valuation purposes only). This means that the remaining balance will be valued based on the prices of more recent purchases

last in first out (LIFO)	this method of inventory valuation assumes that the most recently acquired inventory will be used first, leaving the earlier acquisitions to make up the value of the remaining balance. This does not have to correspond with the actual order of usage
average cost (AVCO)	this inventory valuation method involves calculating a new weighted average cost of goods each time that a new purchase is made, and using this valuation for subsequent issues and balances until further purchases are made
manufacturing account	this cost statement is produced at the end of a period to summarise costs under various categories
direct materials	this is calculated as the total of opening inventory of raw materials, plus materials purchased, minus closing inventory of raw materials
direct cost	the total of direct costs (also known as prime cost) – in a manufacturing account it is calculated by adding direct materials used in manufacture to direct labour
manufacturing cost	a subtotal made up of the total of direct cost (direct materials and direct labour) and manufacturing overheads
cost of goods manufactured	this subtotal is the production costs of goods that have been completed and is made up of manufacturing cost adjusted for inventories of work-in-progress
cost of goods sold	a total based on the factory cost of goods manufactured which has been adjusted for inventories of finished goods

Activities

3.1 You work for a training organisation, and have been asked to work out the answers for an exercise to be set for accountancy students. You are to classify each inventory item on the following list into one of the following categories:
- raw materials
- work-in-progress
- finished goods

List of inventory items for classification:

Inventory item and organisation	Classification
Wood held by a door manufacturer	
Flour held by a cake manufacturer	
Cakes awaiting icing held by a cake manufacturer	
Doors awaiting sanding and polishing held by a door manufacturer	
Flour held by a flour miller	
Wheat held by a flour miller	
Screws held by a screw manufacturer	
Screws held by a door manufacturer	

3.2 Identify the correct inventory valuation method from the characteristics given by putting a tick in the relevant column of the following table.

Characteristic	FIFO	LIFO	AVCO
• Issues of inventory are valued at the weighted average cost of purchases • Inventory is valued at the oldest purchase costs • Issues of inventory are valued at the most recent purchase prices • Inventory is valued at the weighted average cost of purchases • Inventory is valued at the most recent purchase costs • Issues of inventory are valued at the oldest purchase prices			

3.3 Indicate whether the following statements are true or false by putting a tick in the relevant columns of the table below.

	True	False
• FIFO costs issues of inventory in the same order in which it was received • FIFO values closing inventory based on the oldest purchase prices • LIFO costs issues of inventory at the oldest purchase prices • LIFO values closing inventory at the average cost of purchases • AVCO costs issues of inventory at the most recent purchase prices • AVCO values closing inventory at the weighted average cost of purchases		

3.4 Which one of the following is true for the FIFO method of inventory valuation?

(a) Issues are valued at the most recent purchase prices

(b) Inventory is valued at the average of the cost of purchases

(c) A new average cost is calculated each time a purchase is made

(d) Inventory is valued at the most recent purchase prices

Answer (a) or (b) or (c) or (d)

3.5 Which one of the following is true for the LIFO method of inventory valuation?

(a) The latest purchase costs are used to value issues

(b) Issues are valued at the average of the cost of purchases

(c) Inventory remaining at the end of the period is valued at the most recent purchase costs

(d) Issues are unlikely to be valued at the actual cost of purchase

Answer (a) or (b) or (c) or (d)

3.6 Which one of the following is true for the AVCO method of inventory valuation?

(a) Uses the oldest purchase costs to value issues

(b) Inventory valued at the average of the cost of purchases

(c) Issues are valued at the most recent purchase prices

(d) Inventory remaining at the end of the period is valued at the oldest purchase costs

Answer (a) or (b) or (c) or (d)

3.7 Identify which one of the following inventory calculations is correct.

(a) Opening inventory, minus purchases, minus issues, equals closing inventory.

(b) Purchases, minus issues, minus opening inventory, equals closing inventory.

(c) Closing inventory plus opening inventory, equals purchases.

(d) Opening inventory, plus purchases, minus issues, equals closing inventory.

Answer (a) or (b) or (c) or (d)

3.8 Identify which inventory valuation method is being used in the following situation. Choose between FIFO, LIFO, AVCO by ticking the box below.

Receipts			Issues			Balance	
Quantity (units)	Cost per unit	Total cost	Quantity	Value per unit	Total value	Quantity	Total value
100	£20	£2,000				100	£2,000
150	£25	£3,750				250	£5,750
			80	£23	£1,840	170	£3,910

FIFO	
LIFO	
AVCO	

3.9 The following table shows the movements in a certain type of inventory through a business's stores in February.

Date	Receipts Units	Receipts Cost	Issues Units	Issues Cost
Feb 6	100	£600		
Feb 15	150	£1,200		
Feb 22	250	£2,500		
Feb 26			300	
Feb 27	200	£2,400		

Complete the table below for the issue on 26 February and closing inventory values at 28 February.

Method	Cost of issue on 26 February	Closing inventory value at 28 February
FIFO	£2,300	£4,400
LIFO	£2,900	£3,800
AVCO	£2,580	£4,120

3.10 Wyvern Ltd has the following movements in a certain type of inventory into and out of its stores for the month of January:

Date	Receipts		Issues	
	Units	Cost	Units	Cost
3 January	100	£1,000		
14 January	200	£2,400		
20 January	100	£1,400		
22 January			150	
27 January	300	£4,500		

Complete the table below for the issue on 22 January and closing inventory values at 31 January.

Method	Cost of issue on 22 January	Closing inventory value at 31 January
FIFO	£	£
LIFO	£	£
AVCO	£	£

inventory valuation and the manufacturing account 79

3.11 Complete the tables below, using the FIFO, LIFO and AVCO methods of inventory valuation:

(a) FIFO

Receipts			Issues			Balance		
Quantity (units)	Cost per unit	Total cost	Quantity (units)	Value per unit	Total value	Quantity (units)	Value per unit	Total value
						2,000	£2.02	£4,040
10,000	£2.20							
			8,000					

(b) LIFO

Receipts			Issues			Balance		
Quantity (units)	Cost per unit	Total cost	Quantity (units)	Value per unit	Total value	Quantity (units)	Value per unit	Total value
						2,000	£2.02	£4,040
10,000	£2.20							
			8,000					

(c) AVCO

Receipts			Issues			Balance		
Quantity (units)	Cost per unit	Total cost	Quantity (units)	Value per unit	Total value	Quantity (units)	Value per unit	Total value
						2,000	£2.02	£4,040
10,000	£2.20							
			8,000					

3.12 Reorder the following costs into a manufacturing account format on the right-hand side of the table below.

Make sure that the arithmetic of your account is accurate.

	£		£
DIRECT COST	79,000		
Opening inventory of raw materials	13,000		
Direct labour	30,000		
Closing inventory of finished goods	14,000		
COST OF GOODS SOLD	93,000		
Purchases of raw materials	47,000		
Opening inventory of finished goods	15,000		
MANUFACTURING COST	99,000		
Closing inventory of work-in-progress	19,000		
Opening inventory of work-in-progress	12,000		
Closing inventory of raw materials	11,000		
DIRECT MATERIALS USED	49,000		
Manufacturing overheads	20,000		
COST OF GOODS MANUFACTURED	92,000		

3.13 Reorder the following costs into a manufacturing account format on the right-hand side of the table below.

Make sure that the arithmetic of your account is accurate.

	£		£
Closing inventory of finished goods	32,000	Opening inventory of raw materials	15,000
COST OF GOODS SOLD	178,000	Purchases of raw materials	85,000
Manufacturing overheads	38,000		100,000
Opening inventory of raw materials	15,000	Less Closing inventory of raw materials	18,000
DIRECT MATERIALS USED	82,000	DIRECT MATERIALS USED	82,000
Opening inventory of work-in-progress	26,000	Direct labour	55,000
Direct labour	55,000	DIRECT COST	137,000
MANUFACTURING COST	175,000	Manufacturing overheads	38,000
Opening inventory of finished goods	37,000	MANUFACTURING COST	175,000
COST OF GOODS MANUFACTURED	173,000	Add Opening inventory of work-in-progress	26,000
Purchases of raw materials	85,000		201,000
Closing inventory of work-in-progress	28,000	Less Closing inventory of work-in-progress	28,000
DIRECT COST	137,000	COST OF GOODS MANUFACTURED	173,000
Closing inventory of raw materials	18,000	Add Opening inventory of finished goods	37,000
			210,000
		Less Closing inventory of finished goods	32,000
		COST OF GOODS SOLD	178,000

4 Labour costs

this chapter covers...

We have already seen that labour cost is one of the three main elements of cost, along with materials and expenses. In this chapter we will look in more detail at labour costs.

The chapter starts by examining the main ways that employees' pay can be calculated. These are:

- payment based on the normal time worked – known as basic pay
- payment based on extra time worked – known as overtime
- payment of a bonus
- payment based on output – piecework

We will examine features of each method, and carry out calculations.

We will then link this understanding of labour costs to our earlier work on cost classification and coding, with examples of how coding can be used for labour costs.

Finally we will refer to our earlier work on cost behaviour, and identify how the different methods of labour payment affect the behaviour of the labour cost.

METHODS OF CALCULATING PAYMENTS FOR LABOUR

The cost of labour for an organisation is the cost of paying employees for the work that they carry out. There are several different ways that these amounts can be calculated, and the details of the method that applies to each group of employees will have been formally agreed and set out in a contract of employment.

There are four main methods of calculating pay:

- **time rate** – payment based on time worked, also known as **basic rate**
- **overtime** – a form of time rate – payment for extra time worked
- payment of a **bonus** added onto the normal time rate and overtime
- **piecework** – payment based on the amount of work carried out

Organisations may use one method of payment for all employees or they may have different methods for different groups of employees.

We will now examine these four main payment methods that you will need to be familiar with.

time rate

Time rate is based on payment for the amount of time spent working.

Time rate is a very common method of calculating labour payments. The unit of time that is used could be a week or a month, but could alternatively be an hour. Examples of time rate payments could be

- a trainee accountant paid £1,200 per month
- a production supervisor paid £380 per week
- a production operator paid £8.00 per hour

In each case, the contract would state how much time would normally be spent working, for example 38 hours per week.

For both the employee and the organisation, pay based on a time rate means that it is known in advance how much will be paid. This makes planning easier for both employer and employee and gives the employees the security of knowing that they will be paid the same for each period at work.

However, just using this payment method means that efficient employees are paid the same as inefficient ones, and they receive no financial reward for working harder.

The amount paid per time period of normal working is known as the **basic rate**, and this term is commonly used for the normal hourly rate. For example, an employee may be paid a basic rate of £8.00 per hour for each of the 38 hours worked in a week.

overtime rate

An overtime rate is a time rate that is paid for time worked in excess of the normal contracted time.

An overtime rate (usually hourly) is invariably higher than the basic rate. For example a basic rate of £7.00 and an overtime rate of £10.50 per hour.

worked example

Suppose a production operative was entitled to a basic rate of £7.00 per hour, based on a 38 hour week, and an overtime rate of £10.50 per hour for any hours in excess of 38 hours. If during a certain week this person worked 42 hours, then the pay would be calculated as:

Basic rate	38 hours x £7.00	£266.00
Overtime rate	4 hours x £10.50	£42.00
Total		£308.00

bonus payments

A bonus payment is an extra payment paid to employees as a reward for productivity.

Bonus payments are normally offered to reward employees when the organisation performs well, either in term of output (items produced, products sold) or when sales and profit are good.

Bonus payments are based on a variety of calculations, but in this chapter we will concentrate on a simple approach based on the output achieved by the employee. This involves paying a bonus if the employee's work output (for example units of production) is greater than a certain amount. The bonus is calculated based on the extra amount produced.

worked example

Suppose an employee is paid a basic rate of £8.00 per hour for a 35 hour week. A weekly bonus is paid if the average production of an employee is more than 4 units per hour. For every unit produced by the employee in excess of 4 units per hour a bonus of £1.20 is payable.

Suppose that during a certain week an employee works 35 hours and produces 170 units.

The bonus would be calculated as follows:

Actual output	170 units
Expected output (35 hours x 4 units)	140 units
Excess output that earns bonus	30 units
Bonus payable 30 units x £1.20 = £36.00	

This bonus would be paid in addition to the amount paid at the time rate:

Basic rate	35 hours x £8.00	£280.00
Bonus (as calculated above)		£36.00
Total pay		£316.00

If the employee had produced 140 units or fewer then no bonus would be paid, and the person would just receive the time rate based amount. There would be no reduction in pay (or 'negative bonus') for producing fewer than the expected number of units.

A production based bonus system used in conjunction with payment by time rate gives employees the security to know that their pay will not fall below the time-based amount. It also encourages productive working which is beneficial for both employees and the organisation.

piecework

piecework is payment based on the number of items produced by the employee

Payment by 'piecework' is the name given to labour payments that are entirely based on output or production levels. Unlike the methods that we have examined already, piecework schemes do not take account of the time that the employee spends working. Instead, piecework simply makes a payment per unit produced, and this is the only amount that the employee earns.

worked example

Suppose an employee is paid by piecework based on £15 per unit produced.

During the week the employee works 46 hours and produces 28 units.

The employee will be paid £15 x 28 units = £420.00.

Note that the time spent working is not used in the calculation at all.

For the business, the piecework method means that each unit produced has the same labour cost, and payment is only made for productive work. However not all production processes are suitable for payment by piecework, because the output of each employee cannot always be measured.

When piecework is used, the employees' earnings are limited only by the speed of their work, so there is no theoretical limit to how much they can earn. This is likely to make the employee's pay vary week by week.

We will now use a Case Study to illustrate the calculations involved in the payment methods that we have examined.

Case Study

FASHION WORKS: LABOUR COSTS

situation

'Fashion Works' is a small company that manufactures clothes. It uses various payment methods for its employees. The following are details of the payment methods for a sample of employees in different departments for a week.

Cutting Department: basic rate + productivity bonus

Employees who work in the cutting department are paid £8.00 per hour for a 35 hour week.

The employees are also paid a bonus if they complete more than 10 items per hour. The bonus is £0.25 per item completed in excess of this number.

Rashid Patel works in the cutting department. During the week he worked 35 hours and completed 365 items.

Sewing Department: piecework payment

The sewing machinists in the sewing department are paid at a piecework rate of £4.00 per completed item. Stephan Schallert is a sewing machinist. During the week he worked for 40 hours and completed 89 items.

Sales Department: basic rate + overtime

All employees in the sales department are paid £9.00 per hour for a basic week of 35 hours. Any overtime worked is paid at a rate of £13.50 per hour. Sara Lee works in the sales department. During the week Sara worked the basic 35 hours.

required

Calculate the gross pay for each of the employees listed on the previous page.

solution

Cutting Department

Rashid Patel

Time rate: 35 hours x £8.00		£280.00
Bonus calculation:		
Actual output	365 units	
Expected output (35 hours x 10 units)	350 units	
Excess output that earns bonus	15 units	
Bonus payable 15 units x £0.25		£3.75
Total pay		£283.75

Sewing Department

Stephan Schallert

Piecework rate 89 items x £4.00	£356.00
(Hours worked is not relevant)	

Sales Department

Sara Lee

Time rate: basic rate	35 hours x £9.00	£315.00

CLASSIFYING AND CODING LABOUR COSTS

We discovered earlier in this book that labour is one of the three main **elements of cost** (materials, labour and expenses). We also saw that **the nature** of labour costs may be

- **direct** (part of prime cost) or
- **indirect** (part of production overheads or non-production overheads).

Direct labour costs are the costs of employing those who work directly engaged on production. This includes production operatives, but not supervisors or those not directly involved in producing the output of the organisation.

Indirect labour costs are the costs of employing those in the production area who are not directly involved in production, and the cost of employing those who work in other functions (for example administration or selling and distribution).

The following Case Study is developed from the previous Case Study and uses a coding system to classify:

- the **elements** of cost (materials, labour and expenses)
- the **nature** of costs (direct costs, indirect costs)

Case Study

FASHION WORKS: CODING LABOUR COSTS

situation

'Fashion Works' is a small company that manufactures clothes. The gross pay for three sample employees has already been calculated (see previous page), and is summarised below:

Department	Employee	Gross Pay
Cutting	Rashid Patel	£283.75
Sewing	Stephan Schallert	£356.00
Sales	Sara Lee	£315.00

Coding Policy Manual

This internal document includes the following details:

- Sewing and cutting are production activities.
- Each code is made up of three digits:
    - the first digit shows the cost centre or profit centre
    - the second digit shows whether the cost is direct, or indirect
    - the third digit is for the element of cost (materials, labour, expenses)

- Extract from cost centre /profit centre list (first digit of code)
    1   Cutting Department (cost centre)
    2   Sewing Department (cost centre)
    3   Administration Department (cost centre)
    4   Sales Department (profit centre)
- Extract from list of 'nature' analysis codes (second digit of code)
    1   Direct
    2   Indirect
- Extract from list of 'element' analysis codes (third digit of code)
    1   Materials
    2   Labour
    3   Expenses
- Example of a code:

    Direct materials issued to the cutting department would be coded 111.

required

Show the coding relating to each employee's labour cost.

solution

Department	Employee	Gross Pay	Code
Cutting	Rashid Patel	£ 283.75	112
Sewing	Stephan Schallert	£ 356.00	212
Sales	Sara Lee	£ 315.00	422

BEHAVIOUR OF LABOUR COSTS

In Chapter 2 we explained the principles of **cost behaviour.** We identified three basic ways in which costs can behave. The three types of cost are:

- **fixed costs** – costs that do not change when the output changes – eg when the number of items produced increases
- **variable costs** – those costs which change as the level of output (or activity level) changes

- **semi-variable costs** – those costs that contain both a fixed element and a variable element

Now that we have examined labour costs in some detail we will identify how they can be classified, using the above categories. The table shown below summarises the cost behaviour of the main methods of labour payments.

cost behaviour:	Fixed Costs - these do not change with output	Variable Costs - these do change with output	Semi-variable Costs - a mix of fixed and variable costs
example based on labour costs:	Basic rate pay – eg for administrative and sales staff	Piecework payments – eg for production workers not on basic rate pay	Basic rate pay topped up by a production-based bonus

We will now return to the situation in the previous Case Study to apply these principles.

Case Study

FASHION WORKS: LABOUR COST BEHAVIOUR

situation

'Fashion Works' is a small company that manufactures clothes. It uses various payment methods for its employees (see previous Case Studies).

The gross pay for various employees has already been calculated, and is shown below.

Cutting Department

Rashid Patel

Time rate: 35 hours x £8.00		£280.00
Production-based bonus payable 15 units x £0.25		£3.75
Total pay		£283.75

Sewing Department

Stephan Schallert

Piecework rate	89 items x £4.00	£356.00

Sales Department

Sara Lee

Time rate: basic rate   35 hours x £9.00   £315.00

required

Draw up a table, showing the method of payment and the cost behaviour of the labour cost of each employee.

solution

Employee	Method	Cost behaviour
Rashid Patel	Time-based payment with a production-based bonus	Semi-variable
Stephan Schallert	Piecework	Variable
Sara Lee	Time-based payment (basic rate pay only)	Fixed

Chapter Summary

- There are several methods of making labour payments. These include time rates (including basic rates and overtime rates), time rates with bonus systems, and piecework rates.

- Labour costs can be classified and coded based on the categories covered earlier in this book; these include cost and profit centres, direct and indirect costs.

- Labour costs can behave as fixed costs, variable costs, or semi-variable costs, depending on the method of payment.

Key Terms

time rate — the method of remuneration when payment is on the basis of time spent at work; it can be an hourly rate or based on a longer time period

basic rate — a time rate that is applied to the normal contracted work time, and is usually an hourly rate

overtime rate — the rate (normally hourly) paid for time worked in excess of the normal contracted time; it is usually at a higher rate than basic rate

piecework — a payment system when the employee is paid for the work carried out (eg per task or unit); this does not take any account of the time taken

bonus system — a system used in conjunction with another payment method (for example time rate, which provides additional payment for efficient working, eg production that is more than a set level)

Activities

4.1 Which one of the following is a characteristic of the time-rate method of labour payment?

(a) Pay is linked directly to output

(b) Employees earn a guaranteed level of pay

(c) Hard-working employees earn extra on top of basic pay

(d) Pay is calculated as units of output multiplied by the rate per unit

Answer (a) or (b) or (c) or (d)

4.2 Which one of the following is a characteristic of the piecework method of labour payment?

(a) Pay is calculated as hours worked multiplied by hourly rate

(b) Employees are paid an hourly rate plus extra for a higher output than agreed

(c) Pay is unaffected by changes in output

(d) Employees are paid on the basis of output

Answer (a) or (b) or (c) or (d)

4.3 Which one of the following is a characteristic of the time-rate plus bonus method of labour payment?

(a) Wages are linked to output but a set level of pay is guaranteed

(b) Employees are paid on the basis of output

(c) Employees earn a fixed level of pay

(d) Pay is calculated as units of output multiplied by the rate per unit

Answer (a) or (b) or (c) or (d)

4.4 Identify the following statements as true or false by putting a tick in the relevant column of the table below.

	True	False
• Indirect labour costs cannot be identified with the product or service produced		
• Direct labour costs paid on a time-rate basis do not vary directly with the level of activity		
• Indirect labour costs include the wages of office staff		
• Direct labour costs paid on a piecework basis remain fixed at all levels of output		
• Indirect labour costs are a variable cost		
• Direct labour costs include the wages of factory supervisors		

4.5 Identify the labour payment method by putting a tick in the relevant column of the table below.

Payment method	Time-rate	Piecework	Time-rate plus bonus
• Assured amount of pay for time worked, but no extra pay for efficient working			
• Assured amount of pay for time worked, plus possible extra pay based on output			
• No assured amount of pay, but no limit on earnings as pay based on the production of employees			

4.6 Identify one advantage for each labour payment method by putting a tick in the relevant column of the table below.

Payment method	Time-rate	Piecework	Time-rate plus bonus
• Each unit of production has the same labour cost and payment is made only for productive work			
• Both the employee and the business know in advance how much will be paid			
• When the employee works harder than expected an additional payment is made above the time-rate			

4.7 Vulcan Ltd pays a time-rate of £12 per hour to its direct labour for a standard 34 hour week. Any of the labour force working in excess of 34 hours per week is paid an overtime rate of £16 per hour.

Calculate the basic wage, overtime and gross wage for the two workers in the table below.

Worker	Hours worked	Basic wage	Overtime	Gross wage
J Cassidy	38	£	£	£
P Olinski	40	£	£	£

4.8 Clark Ltd uses a piecework method to pay labour in its factory. The rate used is £1.25 per unit produced.

Calculate the gross wage for the week for the two workers in the table below.

Worker	Units produced in week	Gross wage
T Theaker	344	£
K Panayi	428	£

4.9 Benson Ltd uses a time-rate method with bonus to pay its direct labour in its factory. The time-rate used is £11 per hour and a worker is expected to produce 8 units an hour, anything over this and the worker is paid a bonus of £0.50 per unit.

Calculate the basic wage, bonus and gross wage for the three workers in the table below.

Worker	Hours worked	Units produced	Basic wage	Bonus	Gross wage
N Allen	32	284	£	£	£
T Chalabi	36	312	£	£	£
A McCall	40	310	£	£	£

4.10 The following table gives pay data for four employees who work in a factory.

Employee number	Hours worked	Units produced
1	41	440
2	35	400
3	38	300
4	40	420

Calculate the gross pay for each employee based on each of the following alternative payment methods and complete the table below.

(a) Time rate of £9.00 per hour for 35 hour week, with any overtime paid at £12 per hour.

(b) Piecework at £0.95 per unit produced.

(c) Time rate of £10.00 per hour for all hours worked, plus a bonus of £0.50 for each unit produced in excess of 10 per hour.

Employee number	Payment methods		
	(a)	(b)	(c)
1	£	£	£
2	£	£	£
3	£	£	£
4	£	£	£

4.11 Country Cottage Doors Limited has a range of employees who are paid by different methods. The normal working hours for each full time employee are 40 hours per week.

Calculate the basic wage (or piecework), overtime or bonus, and gross wage for the three workers in the table below.

Employee	Basic wage or piecework	Overtime or bonus	Gross wage
John Evans (carpenter) – worked 42 hours – paid £10 per hour – overtime at £15 per hour	£	£	£
Vikram Singh (door polisher) – 12 doors polished – paid £35 per door polished	£	£	£
Julian Winstone (part time cleaner) – worked 12 hours – paid £6.50 per hour	£	£	£
Sara Lewinski (office worker) – paid £350 per week	£	£	£

4.12 Alpha Motors is a garage that sells and services cars. Both sales and servicing are direct activities.

An extract from the company's coding policy manual is as follows:

Each code is made up of three digits:

- the first digit shows the cost centre or profit centre
- the next digit shows whether the cost is direct or indirect
- the next digit shows the element of cost (materials, labour, expenses)

Extract from cost centre / profit centre list (first digit of code):

1 Servicing Department (cost centre)
2 Administration Department (cost centre)
3 Sales Department (profit centre)

Extract from list of analysis codes (second digit of code):

1 Direct
2 Indirect

Extract from list of analysis codes (third digit of code):

1 Materials
2 Labour
3 Expenses

The following employees have pay data for the last week:

- Jane Buchan is a mechanic in the servicing department. She earns £12.00 per hour for a 36 hour week, with overtime paid at £16.00 per hour. Jane worked 39 hours.
- Louis Chowski is also a mechanic in the servicing department with the same pay rates and hours as Jane. He worked 40 hours.
- Jim Wright is a car salesman. He earns a basic £500.00 per week, with a bonus of £40.00 for each car sold. He sold two cars in the week.
- John Rogers is the company administrator. He earns £420.00 per week.

Calculate the gross pay for each employee and show the coding, using the following table.

Employee	Basic pay	Overtime or bonus	Total pay	Code
Jane Buchan	£	£	£	
Louis Chowski	£	£	£	
Jim Wright	£	£	£	
John Rogers	£	£	£	

4.13 At a cake manufacturing factory, the following employees are paid as shown below:

- Bill Brown is a machine operator in the factory and his clock card for last week shows that he worked 38 hours. His hourly rate of pay is £8 per hour.
- Sheila Williams is a skilled nutritionist, designing new products and her clock card shows that she worked 44 hours. Her hourly rate of pay is £11 per hour, with overtime for hours worked beyond 40 hours per week at a rate of £16.50 per hour.
- Sonja Patel is a production supervisor. She is paid a weekly rate of £430 per week.

labour costs   99

An extract from the company's coding policy manual is as follows:

Each code is made up of three digits:
- the first digit shows the cost centre
- the next digit shows whether the cost is direct or indirect
- the next digit shows the element of cost (materials, labour, expenses)

Extract from cost centre list:
1   Factory
2   Product design
3   Offices

Extract from list of analysis codes (second digit):
1   Direct
2   Indirect

Extract from list of analysis codes (third digit):
1   Materials
2   Labour
3   Expenses

Calculate the gross pay for each employee and show the coding, using the following table.

Employee	Basic pay	Overtime	Total pay	Code
Bill Brown	£	£	£	
Sheila Williams	£	£	£	
Sonja Patel	£	£	£	

5 Providing information and using spreadsheets

this chapter covers...

This chapter commences with some examples of cost reports that can be used to provide information.

We will then go on to examine budgets and the part they play in the management of an organisation. We will describe:

- how budgets can be used to help monitor and control the costs of an organisation
- variances – the differences between budgeted and actual income and costs
- the need to be able to identify 'adverse' and 'favourable' variances
- the need to be able to identify 'significant' variances based on definitions that are provided

The rest of the chapter is then used to examine how spreadsheets can be used to present costing information. This starts with an overview of spreadsheets including some important terms, and is followed by a section on how information can be presented.

We then look at how formulas can be used in spreadsheets to carry out calculations automatically. This includes using normal arithmetical functions as well as some alternative ways to produce totals, averages and percentages.

The chapter concludes with a brief section on sorting data.

SOME COMMON COST REPORTS

Information may be required in a wide variety of forms and with a range of content. We will now examine some of the more common requests and formats for cost reports that you may come across.

unit cost reports

You may be presented with information about the total costs of producing a certain number of products, and asked to calculate the cost for producing one unit (the 'unit cost'). This is normally a straight forward calculation, and involves:

- calculating the total costs for each category of cost (for example each element) based on the given production level

- dividing these totals by the production level to arrive at unit costs for each category of cost

- adding these unit costs together to arrive at a total unit cost

worked example

A manufacturer has the following cost information for a production level of 30,000 units:

Direct materials	15,000 kilos at £15 per kilo
Direct labour	9,000 hours at £10 per hour
Expenses	£60,000 in total

If we are asked to calculate the unit costs by element and in total, the calculation would be as follows.

	Total Cost (30,000 units)	Unit Cost
Materials	15,000 x £15 = £225,000	£7.50
Labour	9,000 x £10 = £90,000	£3.00
Expenses	£60,000	£2.00
Total	£375,000	£12.50

Note that in this example we also calculated the total cost for 30,000 units of £375,000. This gives us a useful check, since £375,000 divided by 30,000 units is £12.50, which agrees with the total of the unit cost column.

It may be worth remembering that a unit cost is another way of expressing 'cost per unit'. The use of the word 'per' is an indication that the calculation can be carried out by dividing the cost by the units, as we have here. This logic will apply to any calculation – for example 'miles per hour' is calculated by dividing miles travelled by hours taken.

cost reports using cost behaviour

Another common request may be to calculate the costs (total cost and/or cost per unit) for one or more production levels where we are provided with information on the cost behaviour. We saw in Chapter 2 how cost behaviour could be used to help with calculations because:

- **fixed costs** will remain the same in total at different production levels, but
- **variable costs** will change directly in line with production levels.

The following example will remind us of how these calculations can be carried out.

worked example

A company is costing a single product, and has the following information available:

Variable costs per unit:

    Materials £5

    Labour £2

Fixed costs: £60,000

The production level may be 12,000 units, or it may be 15,000.

Suppose we have been asked to calculate the total costs and the unit costs at each of these production levels, using a table.

	12,000 units		15,000 units	
	Total Cost	Unit Cost	Total Cost	Unit Cost
Materials	£60,000	£5	£75,000	£5
Labour	£24,000	£2	£30,000	£2
Fixed costs	£60,000	£5	£60,000	£4
Total	£144,000	£12	£165,000	£11

Notice that the unit costs for variable costs remain the same at different production levels, but the unit costs for fixed costs reduce as the production level increases.

BUDGETS – COMPARING ACTUAL AND EXPECTED INCOME AND COSTS

In order to help make sense of the information provided, it is often useful to compare it with what was expected. Expected income and costs will often have been calculated previously as part of a **budget**.

what is a budget?

A budget is a financial plan for an organisation that is prepared in advance.

A budget is an important part of the planning process that needs to be carried out by managers. It will be based on:

- the products that will be made (or services provided)
- the number of products that will be made (or services provided) and sold

A budget will also calculate the expected costs of the organisation, often analysed into the various classifications that we have studied earlier in this book.

what are the purposes of a budget?

The main purposes of a budget are as follows, although organisations may place different emphasis on the various purposes to suit their needs.

- **the budget creates plans**

    By producing a budget, managers can ensure that they have achievable plans that have been properly agreed. They will know what they need to do to achieve those plans.

- **the budget communicates and coordinates the plans**

    Each manager in the organisation needs to know what the plans are and what their part is in fulfilling these plans. They must all work together using the same overall plan.

- **the budget can be used to monitor and control**

    An important reason for producing a budget is so that the actual results can be monitored against the budget. This will enable action to be taken where necessary to achieve the required result.

The key features of a budget that we should remember is that

- the budget helps with **planning**
- it can also be used to **monitor** and **control** what actually happens

It is this concept of **monitoring** and **control** that is very important when managing an organisation.

standard costs

You may come across the term 'standard costs' in relation to a budget. Just like budgeted costs, standard costs are expected costs that have been calculated in advance.

Whereas budgets tend to be used for total income and costs for a period, standard costs are calculated for individual units of output – for example an individual product or service. Not every organisation creates standard costs for their products, but where they are available they can then be used to help create budgets.

You may find that the term 'budgeted / standard costs' (or something similar) is used to describe expected costs in an activity or assessment task. Whatever term is used to describe expected costs, they are used in the same way to make comparisons with actual costs and calculate variances, as we will now see.

calculating variances

In order to monitor and control costs we need to compare actual costs with budgeted costs. We will carry this out for each type of cost, and calculate any differences between the budget figures and the actual figures. These differences are known as **variances** and can be either:

- **adverse** – where the actual cost is greater than the budgeted cost, or
- **favourable** – where the actual cost is less than the budgeted cost.

These descriptions of variances are fairly self-explanatory; adverse variances are 'bad news', whereas favourable variances are 'good news'. These variances for costs are always calculated as:

> budgeted cost *minus* actual cost

If the answer is positive, the variance is favourable; if the answer is negative the variance is adverse.

worked example

If budgeted material costs for a month were £85,000, but the actual material costs were £93,000, then the material variance would be £8,000 adverse. This is calculated as £85,000 - £93,000 = -£8,000. Notice that the negative answer confirms that it is an adverse variance, although this should be clear from the figures since the actual cost is greater.

If we were calculating the variances for income, then if the actual income were greater than budgeted income this would create a favourable variance – i.e. the calculation would be the other way around.

Case Study

MONITOR LIMITED: CALCULATING VARIANCES

situation

You work for Monitor Limited, a company that manufactures speed cameras. One of your duties is to calculate variances based on the monthly variance report of budgeted and actual income and costs. The latest (partly completed) report is shown below.

	Budget £	Actual £	Variance £	Adverse or Favourable
Income	280,000	275,000		
Direct Materials	47,500	49,200		
Direct Labour	59,800	66,400		
Production Overheads	74,200	73,600		
Administration Overheads	35,900	36,900		
Selling and Distribution Overheads	28,400	24,700		

required

Complete the report, showing variances and whether each variance is adverse or favourable.

solution

	Budget £	Actual £	Variance £	Adverse or Favourable
Income	280,000	275,000	5,000	Adverse
Direct Materials	47,500	49,200	1,700	Adverse
Direct Labour	59,800	66,400	6,600	Adverse
Production Overheads	74,200	73,600	600	Favourable
Administration Overheads	35,900	36,900	1,000	Adverse
Selling and Distribution Overheads	28,400	24,700	3,700	Favourable

identifying significant variances

Some variances may be considered **significant** – these are the ones that managers will probably want to investigate most thoroughly. You may be asked to identify (to point out) significant variances, and you would be told how to decide whether any variances were significant or not. There are two main methods of identifying significant variances. Both are quite straightforward, but care is needed in the calculation.

- **Is the variance greater than a given amount?** For example, variances over £5,000 may be considered significant. This could be different for each type of variance – for example adverse variances over £6,000 could be considered significant, but favourable variances might have to be over £8,000.

- **Is the variance greater than a given percentage of the expected figure?** – usually the budget figure that we are comparing the current figure with. For example, a variance greater than 5% of the budget figure could be considered significant. Again, care is needed with the calculation.

calculating percentages of budget figures

When we are presented with actual data and budgeted data, then the variance can be calculated, as we have already seen. To check whether this variance is greater than a given percentage of the budget figure, one method of calculation is to:

1   Divide the variance (ignoring its sign) by the budget figure.

2   Multiply the answer by 100 (or press % on your calculator).

3   Compare this answer with the given percentage.

worked example

Suppose actual direct labour costs for September are £14,720, and the budgeted figure is £14,000. You are asked whether the variance is significant, and told that significant variances are greater than 5% of the budgeted figure.

We firstly calculate the variance as budgeted costs – actual costs.

Variance is £14,000 – £14,720 = minus £720

Then (ignoring the minus sign), divide this figure by the budgeted figure and multiply the answer by 100.

(£720 ÷ £14,000) x 100 = 5.14%

This is greater than 5%, so the variance is significant.

Notice that if we had divided the variance by the actual figure by mistake we would have produced an incorrect answer of less than 5%, which would not be significant.

Please note that when carrying out these calculations you will need to read the instructions very thoroughly, and carry out your calculations carefully.

We will now use the data from the last Case Study to identify significant variances.

MONITOR LIMITED: IDENTIFYING SIGNIFICANT VARIANCES

Case Study

situation

You have already calculated variances based on comparisons between last month's budgeted and actual costs. Your manager now asks you to identify which of the variances are significant.

He tells you that significant variances are those in excess of 10% of budget. This applies to both favourable and adverse variances.

required

He asks you to

(a) calculate for each type of cost the percentage of the variance in relation to the budgeted figure, to two decimal places

(b) complete the final column in the performance report by stating whether each variance is 'significant' or not 'significant'

solution

(a) **variance percentage – workings**

Income	$\dfrac{5{,}000}{280{,}000}$	x	100	=	1.79%
Direct materials	$\dfrac{1{,}700}{47{,}500}$	x	100	=	3.58%
Direct labour	$\dfrac{6{,}600}{59{,}800}$	x	100	=	11.04%
Production overheads	$\dfrac{600}{74{,}200}$	x	100	=	0.81%
Administration overheads	$\dfrac{1{,}000}{35{,}900}$	x	100	=	2.79%
Selling & distribution overheads	$\dfrac{3{,}700}{28{,}400}$	x	100	=	13.03%

(b)

Cost Type	Budget £	Actual £	Variance £	Adverse or favourable	Significant or not significant
Income	280,000	275,000	5,000	Adverse	Not significant
Direct materials	47,500	49,200	1,700	Adverse	Not significant
Direct labour	59,800	66,400	6,600	Adverse	Significant
Production overheads	74,200	73,600	600	Favourable	Not significant
Administration overheads	35,900	36,900	1,000	Adverse	Not significant
Selling and distribution overheads	28,400	24,700	3,700	Favourable	Significant

USING SPREADSHEETS

Spreadsheets are a type of computer software which is particularly useful for various aspects of costing. One of the most commonly used spreadsheets is Microsoft 'Excel', but there are others which work in a similar way. You don't need to use any one particular make of software to study this unit.

A spreadsheet has a grid structure, made up of individual 'boxes' called cells. Along the top of the grid are column letters, and down the left side of the grid are row numbers. Each cell is identified by its location. This is done by referring to the column letter (located directly above the cell), and the row number (located horizontally to the left of the cell).

For example, a cell identified as F7 would be found in the location shown on the following screen image. This identification is also known as the address of the cell.

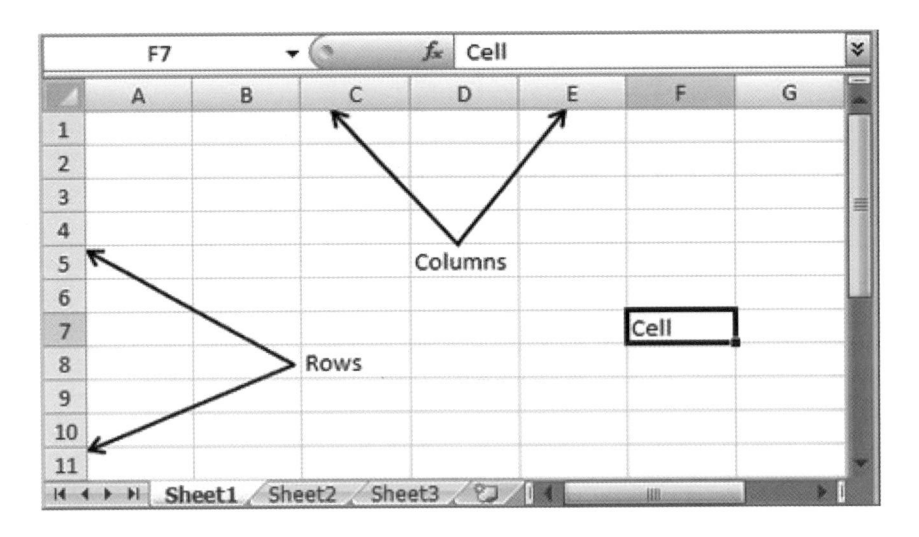

Each cell can be used to contain numbers or words that the user has inserted manually, but can alternatively be used for the automatic result of a formula that has been set up. We will see how some useful formulas are created a little later in this chapter.

some spreadsheet terms

We have already used the term 'cell' to describe a location in a spreadsheet that may contain numbers or words etc. The following are a few other terms that you may need to understand.

- Worksheet – this is the name given to each 'page' of a spreadsheet. These pages will often be originally named as simply 'Sheet 1' etc, but can be easily renamed to suit the user (for example 'Direct costs 20X6').

- Workbook – this is a collection of worksheets which are all held together as one file within the folders held on the computer. The filename is created to suit the user (for example 'Budget 20X6') when the spreadsheet is saved.

- Password – this is a 'word' made up of letters and / or numbers which the user can link to a spreadsheet workbook. The password should only be known to authorised users, and once set up, the workbook can only be opened by keying in the password.

presenting information using a spreadsheet

Much of the information that we use in costing naturally falls into columns and rows. Many of the tables that we used throughout this book are collections of columns and rows, and these could easily be presented by using a spreadsheet. As we will see later, the inclusion of totals for our columns and / or rows is very easy when using a spreadsheet.

When presenting information using a spreadsheet we need to make sure that it is easy to understand – not just for us, but also for anyone who would need to use it. To do this there are a few simple rules that should be followed.

- The title of the spreadsheet should be clearly stated. This should be an unambiguous form of words that tells the reader what the spreadsheet is all about. 'Budget figures' would not be very helpful, whereas 'Budgeted and Actual Costs December 20X6' would be better. The title would normally be placed across the top of the spreadsheet page. If there are several worksheets, one could be called 'December 20X6' while the filename of the whole spreadsheet might be 'Budgeted and Actual Costs 20X6'.

- Each column should normally have a heading at the top which tells the reader what the data in the column represents. An example would be 'Budget Costs £'. Notice that by putting a £ sign at the top of the column it avoids the need to put one in front of each figure in the column.

- Each horizontal row should also have a description, and this is normally placed to the left of the columns that are used for data. If you are creating a spreadsheet for the first time, make sure that you leave a column for this purpose. The description should be clear and tell the reader what will be found in the horizontal row to the right of the description. An example could be 'Direct Materials'.

- If totals are required these can be placed in a column and / or a row with a suitable heading or description as described above.

The following is how a spreadsheet page could look. The title has been omitted here for simplicity.

	A	B	C	D	E
1		Budget £	Actual £	Variance £	A / F
2	Direct materials				
3	Direct labour				
4	Overheads				
5	Totals				

Case Study

FORMAT LIMITED:
PRESENTING SPREADSHEET INFORMATION

A company has produced the following cost information for a product:

Variable costs per unit:
    Materials   £5
    Labour   £4

Fixed costs: £40,000

A spreadsheet has been partly completed to record the total costs at various production levels.

	A	B	C	D	E
1	Number of units				
2		Total costs £	Total costs £	Total costs £	Total costs £
3	Variable materials				
4	Variable labour	40,000	48,000	60,000	72,000
5	Fixed costs				
6	Totals				

required

(a) Insert column headings into each of the cells B1, C1, D1 and E1.
(b) Insert appropriate figures into the remaining cells.

solution

The first step is to work out how many units should head up each column. This is carried out by dividing each total variable labour cost shown by £4 (the unit variable labour cost.

Next the units are used to calculate the variable material costs. The fixed costs are then inserted, and the totals calculated.

	A	B	C	D	E
1	Number of units	10,000	12,000	15,000	18,000
2		Total costs £	Total costs £	Total costs £	Total costs £
3	Variable materials	50,000	60,000	75,000	90,000
4	Variable labour	40,000	48,000	60,000	72,000
5	Fixed costs	40,000	40,000	40,000	40,000
6	Totals	130,000	148,000	175,000	202,000

using basic formulas for calculations

Formulas can be used to automatically calculate the data within a cell. The formula can be entered directly into the cell. As this is carried out, the formula will also appear in the 'formula bar' which is displayed at the top of the spreadsheet page.

Formulas start with the equals sign '=' and can then use cell references together with the following arithmetical and other signs to form an unambiguous instruction for the software.

- Addition: +
- Subtraction: -
- Multiplication: *
- Division: /

An example of a simple formula is:

=F6+F7

which instructs the software to enter into the relevant cell the result of adding the contents of cell F6 to the contents of cell F7.

Formulas can also use numbers in combination with cell references, for example:

=F6*2

which is an instruction to multiply the contents of cell F6 by 2.

Brackets ( ) are also used to instruct the software to deal with the calculation within the brackets first.

For example, if we wish to add together the contents of cells F6 and F7, before multiplying the result by 2 we would use the formula:

=(F6+F7)*2

If the brackets were omitted the software would multiply the contents of cell F7 by 2, and then add the contents of cell F6. This is because the order that the calculation is carried out is always as follows:

- Firstly – any calculation contained in brackets
- Secondly – any multiplication and / or division
- Thirdly – any addition and / or subtraction

We will now use the previous case study to see one way that we could have used formulas for working out the column totals.

Case Study

FORMAT LIMITED: USING FORMULAS FOR ADDITION

The following spreadsheet has been created to show total costs of a product at various production levels.

	A	B	C	D	E
1	Number of units	10,000	12,000	15,000	18,000
2		Total costs £	Total costs £	Total costs £	Total costs £
3	Variable materials	50,000	60,000	75,000	90,000
4	Variable labour	40,000	48,000	60,000	72,000
5	Fixed costs	40,000	40,000	40,000	40,000
6	Totals	130,000	148,000	175,000	202,000

required

Show the formulas that could be used in cells B6, C6, D6 and E6 to total the relevant columns.

solution

The formulas are as follows:

Cell B6:	=B3+B4+B5
Cell C6:	=C3+C4+C5
Cell D6:	=D3+D4+D5
Cell E6:	=E3+E4+E5

Notice that we are only adding the amounts (in £) shown below row 2. For obvious reasons we are ignoring the number of units in row 1 and the headings in row 2. All the formulas here look similar because we are repeating the same pattern each time.

These are not the only formulas that we could use to get these results. The next section examines some alternatives.

providing information and using spreadsheets

Note that in an assessment where there are various formulas that will achieve the same result, marks will be awarded for any valid formula.

Case Study

OVERSEE LIMITED: USING FORMULAS FOR SUBTRACTION

Oversee Limited uses a spreadsheet to present budgeted and actual data and calculate profit and variances. The following spreadsheet has been partly completed.

	A	B	C	D	E
1		Budget £	Actual £	Variance £	A / F
2	Income	130,000	145,000		
3	Direct materials	29,500	31,600		
4	Direct labour	44,100	43,000		
5	Overheads	21,500	24,300		
6	Total costs	95,100	98,900		
7	Profit				

required

- Enter A or F into each cell in column E to denote adverse or favourable variances
- Enter appropriate formulas into the cells in column D to calculate variances, and into the remaining cells in row 7 to calculate profit.

solution

	A	B	C	D	E
1		Budget £	Actual £	Variance £	A / F
2	Income	130,000	145,000	=C2-B2	F
3	Direct materials	29,500	31,600	=C3-B3	A
4	Direct labour	44,100	43,000	=B4-C4	F
5	Overheads	21,500	24,300	=C5-B5	A
6	Total costs	95,100	98,900	=C6-B6	A
7	Profit	=B2-B6	=C2-C6	=C7-B7	F

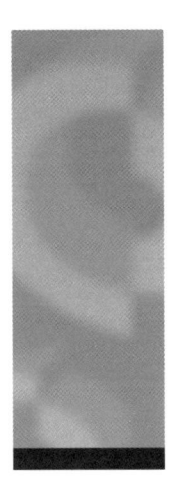

The variance for profit is shown as favourable since the actual profit is greater than the budgeted profit.

Note that here the variance formulas have been developed based on the data so that the answer is always positive. An alternative approach would be to use the same order for each variance (for example the cell in column B minus the cell in column C), and set the spreadsheet to ignore the sign of the calculated variance.

Note also that the formula for the profit variance is able to refer to cells which themselves contain formulas.

There are other formulas that could be used in this case study to achieve the same results.

'SUM' function

We can use 'functions' that are built into the software to simplify some formulas. The 'SUM' function is used to total the content of a number of cells.

The SUM function is used as follows. The equal sign is followed by 'SUM', and this is followed by brackets containing the cell references to be added. The cell references are separated by commas.

This means that: =SUM(B3,B4,B5)

will give the same result as =B3+B4+B5

Where the cells are in the same column or the same row, the formula can be shortened by using the first and last cell references, with a colon ':' between.

For example: =SUM(B3:B5)

This means that all the cells between B3 and B5 would be included.

This is called a range of cells.

'AUTOSUM' function

You may have noticed the 'Σ' in the Excel toolbar. This symbol represents the 'AUTOSUM' function which creates a total using 'SUM' and also suggests which cells should be used to create the total.

To use this function, the cell is first highlighted, and then the 'Σ' symbol in the toolbar is clicked. This will create a 'SUM' formula with a range of cells that the software suggests. The range is also displayed with a dotted rectangle around the cells. If this is the range that is required, the RETURN key is pressed. If the range needs to be changed the dotted rectangle can be moved using the mouse until it encloses the correct cells.

'AVERAGE' function

The AVERAGE function will calculate the simple average of the contents of a number of cells by adding them together and dividing the result by the number of cells. The brackets can either contain all the cells separated by commas, or the first and last in a range, divided by a colon. This is the same layout as the SUM function.

The formula	=AVERAGE(B3:B5)
would give the same result as	=(B3+B4+B5)/3
and could also be shown as	=AVERAGE(B3,B4,B5)

calculating percentages

If we want the result of a calculation to be expressed as a percentage instead of a decimal, then there are two different ways in which this can be achieved.

- the formula for the cell can be expressed with '%' at the end. For example if we want to calculate the contents of cell F6 as a percentage of the contents of cell G6 the formula can be written as =F6/G6%. The answer using this method is displayed as a number, but without a % sign. The % sign should be used in the column heading to make it clear that the data is a percentage.

- if using Excel the formula can firstly be written without the % sign. Then with the cell highlighted 'format' from the toolbar is selected, followed by 'number', 'cell' and then 'percentage'. This will also provide the option to round the answer to a specific number of decimal places at the same time. The answer will then be displayed as a number, followed by the % sign.

Case Study

FUNCTION LIMITED: USING AVERAGES AND PERCENTAGES

Function Limited has a section in which four employees work. Each employee is paid a basic £9 for each hour worked. In addition a bonus of £3 is paid for each unit produced in excess of 2 units per hour worked.

During a specific week the employees had the following data.

Employee	Hours Worked	Units Produced
M. Fletcher	38	85
S. Khan	40	91
P. Smythe	37	78
N. Cathay	40	86

The following spreadsheet is used to present the amount of pay and to calculate further information.

	A	B	C	D	E	F	G
1		M. Fletcher £	S. Khan £	P. Smythe £	N.Cathay £	Section Total £	Average Pay £
2	Basic pay						
3	Bonus						
4	Total pay						
5		%	%	%	%	%	
6	Bonus % of total						

Column G is used to show the average pay details of an employee in the section.

Row 6 is used to show what the bonus paid is as a percentage of total pay for each employee, and for the section.

required

- enter the pay data into rows 2, 3 and 4 for the individual employees only
- enter appropriate formulas into the relevant remaining cells to provide the required information

Enter all the figures in whole pounds.

solution

	A	B	C	D	E	F	G
1		M. Fletcher £	S. Khan £	P. Smythe £	N.Cathay £	Section Total £	Average Pay £
2	Basic pay	342	360	333	360	=SUM(B2:E2)	=AVERAGE(B2:E2)
3	Bonus	27	33	12	18	=SUM(B3:E3)	=AVERAGE(B3:E3)
4	Total pay	369	393	345	378	=SUM(B4:E4)	=AVERAGE(B4:E4)
5		%	%	%	%	%	
6	Bonus % of total	=B3/B4%	=C3/C4%	=D3/D4%	=E3/E4%	=F3/F4%	

Note that other formulas could be used to achieve the same results.

sorting data

The final spreadsheet function that we need to understand and use is the ability to place a column (or row) of data in ascending or descending order. This is based on the content of each cell.

- **Ascending** order places any words into alphabetical order (A followed by B etc), and any numbers into increasing order - from the smallest to the largest (1 followed by 2 etc).
- **Descending** order is the opposite (Z is followed by Y etc) and (for example) 999 would be followed by 998.

There are built in 'sort' tools in the toolbar of Excel, as illustrated below which make this process very easy. When using Excel the column or row which is to be sorted is first highlighted, and then the appropriate toolbar button is clicked.

If there are adjacent columns that also need to move to reflect the new order these will need to be linked by 'associating' them with the original column. However in an assessment it is likely that such a link will be carried out automatically.

Chapter Summary

- Comparisons of actual data with budgeted figures make the actual data more useful for planning and decision making. Differences between actual and budgeted data (called 'variances') can be calculated in monetary and percentage terms, and significant differences can be identified and acted upon.

- Spreadsheets can be used to present costing information. The data can be input directly into cells arranged in rows and columns.

- Formulas can also be used in spreadsheets to make automatic calculations. They can be used for adding, subtracting, multiplying and dividing. Alternative functions can be used to calculate totals, averages and percentages.

- The data in spreadsheet cells can be arranged into ascending or descending order by using 'sort' functions.

Key Terms

budget — a financial planning document that is prepared in advance, and can be used to help monitor and control costs

variances — the difference between the actual data and the budgeted data

adverse variances — these are 'bad news'
- in a performance report when the actual income is lower than budget
- in a performance report when the actual cost is higher than budget

favourable variances — these are 'good news'
- in a performance report when the actual cost is lower than budget
- in a performance report when when the actual income is higher than budget

significant variance — a variance that is brought to the managers' attention for further investigation due to either its high monetary value or the high percentage of the variance from the budget data

spreadsheet — computer software that provides a grid structure that can be used for inputting data and formulas

cell — a single 'box' on a spreadsheet that can contain data

worksheet — one page of a spreadsheet file

workbook — a collection of spreadsheet worksheets that is held as a single file

formula — an instruction contained within a cell to carry out a calculation

Activities

5.1 A manufacturer has the following cost information for a production level of 20,000 units:

Direct materials   12,000 kilos at £25 per kilo

Direct labour   4,000 hours at £10 per hour

Indirect expenses   £60,000 in total

Calculate the unit costs by element and in total, using the following table.

Element	Total Cost (20,000 units)	Unit Cost
Materials	£	£
Labour	£	£
Expenses	£	£
Total	£	£

5.2 A company is costing a single product, and has the following information available:

Variable costs per unit:

Materials   £8

Labour   £5

Total fixed costs   £60,000

The production level may be 10,000 units, or it may be 15,000.

Complete the following table.

	10,000 units		15,000 units	
	Total Cost	Unit Cost	Total Cost	Unit Cost
Materials	£	£	£	£
Labour	£	£	£	£
Fixed Costs	£	£	£	£
Total	£	£	£	£

5.3 Lynx Ltd makes a single product and for a production level of 24,000 units has the following costs:

Material 6,000 kilos at £20 per kilo

Labour 8,000 hours at £12 an hour

Overheads £48,000

Complete the table below to show the unit cost at the production level of 24,000 units.

Element	Unit Cost
Material	£
Labour	£
Overheads	£
Total	£

5.4 Mason Ltd makes a single product and for a production level of 12,000 units has the following costs:

Material 10,000 kilos at £6 per kilo

Labour 7,200 hours at £10 an hour

Overheads £48,000

Complete the table below to show the unit cost at the production level of 12,000 units.

Element	Unit Cost
Material	£
Labour	£
Overheads	£
Total	£

5.5 Identify the following statements as being true or false by putting a tick in the relevant column of the table below.

	True	False
• An adverse variance means budgeted costs are greater than actual costs		
• A variance is the difference between budgeted and actual cost		

5.6 Identify the following statements as being true or false by putting a tick in the relevant column of the table below.

	True	False
• A favourable variance means budgeted costs are less than actual costs		
• If actual costs are greater than budgeted costs the variance is adverse		

5.7 Unicorn Ltd has produced a performance report detailing budgeted and actual cost for last month.

Calculate the amount of the variance for each cost type and then determine whether it is adverse or favourable by putting a tick in the relevant column of the table below.

Cost Type	Budget £	Actual £	Variance	Adverse	Favourable
Direct Materials	45,400	50,200	£		
Direct Labour	28,700	28,200	£		
Production Overheads	19,300	20,200	£		
Administration Overheads	6,800	6,700	£		
Selling and Distribution Overheads	8,700	9,200	£		

5.8 Caldwell Ltd has produced a performance report detailing budgeted and actual cost for last month.

Calculate the amount of the variance for each cost type and then determine whether it is adverse or favourable by putting a tick in the relevant column of the table below.

Cost Type	Budget £	Actual £	Variance	Adverse	Favourable
Direct Materials	15,400	14,900	£		
Direct Labour	20,300	21,200	£		
Production Overheads	11,100	10,700	£		
Administration Overheads	7,600	7,800	£		
Selling and Distribution Overheads	4,900	4,600	£		

5.9 The following performance report for last month has been produced for Hamblin Ltd as summarised in the table below. Any variance in excess of 5% of budget is considered to be significant and should be reported to the relevant manager for review and appropriate action.

Examine the variances in the table below and indicate whether they are significant or not significant by putting a tick in the relevant column.

Cost Type	Budget	Variance	Adverse/ Favourable	Significant	Not Significant
Direct Materials	£40,000	£2,500	Adverse		
Direct Labour	£27,500	£1,250	Favourable		
Production Overheads	£21,000	£1,000	Adverse		
Administration Overheads	£7,500	£500	Adverse		
Selling and Distribution Overheads	£6,500	£750	Favourable		

5.10 The following performance report for last month has been produced for Waring Ltd as summarised in the table below. Any variance in excess of 10% of budget is deemed to be significant and should be reported to the relevant manager for review and appropriate action.

Examine the variances in the table below and indicate whether they are significant or not significant by putting a tick in the relevant column.

Cost Type	Budget	Variance	Adverse/ Favourable	Significant	Not Significant
Direct Materials	£84,000	£8,000	Adverse		
Direct Labour	£53,000	£2,500	Favourable		
Production Overheads	£26,500	£3,000	Adverse		
Administration Overheads	£12,500	£1,500	Adverse		
Selling and Distribution Overheads	£15,500	£1,000	Favourable		

5.11 Hardy Ltd has produced a performance report detailing budgeted and actual cost for last month.

Complete the table on the next page by:
- calculating the amount of the variance for each cost type
- determining whether the variance is adverse or favourable
- determining whether the variance is significant or not significant

For Hardy Ltd significant variances are those in excess of 5% of budget

Cost Type	Budget £	Actual £	Variance	Adverse/ Favourable	Significant/ Not significant
Direct Materials	68,500	64,200	£		
Direct Labour	39,100	40,800	£		
Production Overheads	34,700	33,600	£		
Administration Overheads	45,900	51,000	£		
Selling and Distribution Overheads	28,000	25,100	£		

5.12 A company has produced the following partial cost information for a product:

Variable costs per unit:

    Materials   £8

    Labour   £2

A spreadsheet has been partly completed to record the total costs at various production levels.

	A	B	C	D	E
1	Number of units	Variable Materials £	Variable Labour £	Fixed Costs £	Total Costs £
2			20,000	50,000	
3		120,000			
4			40,000		
5		200,000		50,000	

Required:

- Insert the number of units into each of the cells A2, A3, A4 and A5.
- Insert appropriate figures into the remaining cells in columns B, C and D.
- Insert appropriate formulas into the cells in column E.

5.13 A company has produced the following cost information for a product:

Variable costs per unit:

    Materials   £10

    Labour   £5

    Fixed costs: £28,000

A spreadsheet has been partly completed to automatically record the total costs at various production levels.

	A	B	C	D	E
1	Number of units	Variable Materials £	Variable Labour £	Fixed Costs £	Total Costs £
2	5,000				
3	7,500				
4	10,000				

Complete the spreadsheet using **only formulas** in all cells.

5.14 Manage Limited uses a spreadsheet to present budgeted and actual data and calculate profit and variances. The following spreadsheet has been partly completed.

	A	B	C	D	E
1		Budget £	Actual £	Variance £	A /F
2	Income	210,000	206,000		
3	Materials	44,500	44,600		
4	Labour	63,100	62,000		
5	Overheads	70,500	74,300		
6	Profit				

Required:

- Enter A or F into each cell in column E to denote adverse or favourable variances
- Enter appropriate formulas into the cells in column D to calculate variances, and into the remaining cells in row 6 to calculate profit.

128 introduction to costing tutorial

5.15 Analysis Limited has a section in which four employees work. Each employee is paid a basic £8 for each hour worked. In addition a bonus of £2 is paid for each unit produced in excess of 4 units per hour worked.

During a specific week the employees had the following data.

Employee	Hours Worked	Units Produced
Jo King	36	150
Shelley Beach	40	175
Justin Case	37	160
Cliff Topp	39	172

The following spreadsheet is used to present the amount of pay and to calculate further information.

	A	B	C	D	E	F	G
1		Jo King £	Shelley Beach £	Justin Case £	Cliff Topp £	Section Total £	Average Pay £
2	Basic pay						
3	Bonus						
4	Total pay						
5		%	%	%	%	%	
6	Bonus % of total pay						

Required:

- enter the pay data into rows 2, 3 and 4 for the individual employees only
- calculate and insert the appropriate amounts in cells F2, G2 and B6 only
- enter appropriate formulas into the relevant remaining cells to provide the required information

Answers to activities

CHAPTER 1: THE COSTING SYSTEM

1.1 (d)

1.2 (c)

1.3 (a)

1.4

	True	False
• Management accounting must comply with company law		✓
• Financial accounting provides information for owners and investors	✓	
• Management accounting is based on future events	✓	
• Financial accounting only provides information about what may happen in the future		✓

1.5

Characteristic	Financial Accounting	Management Accounting
• It is based on future events		✓
• Its purpose is to provide information for managers		✓
• It complies with accounting rules	✓	
• It is based on past events	✓	

1.6

Cost	Material	Labour	Overheads
Tubular steel	✓		
Wages of employee operating the moulding machine which produces the chair seats		✓	
Rates of factory			✓
Travel expenses of sales staff			✓
Plastic for making chair seats	✓		
Factory heating and lighting			✓

1.7

Cost	Direct	Indirect
• Flour used to bake bread	✓	
• Rent of bakery		✓
• Wages of bakers	✓	
• Repairs to baking machinery		✓
• Currants used in buns	✓	
• Wages of bakery cleaner		✓
• Insurance of bakery		✓
• Salary of production manager		✓

1.8

Cost	Production	Administration	Selling and distribution
Wages of employees working on the bottling line	✓		
Insurance of delivery lorries			✓
Cost of bottles	✓		
Safety goggles for bottling line employees	✓		
Advertisement for new employees		✓	
Depreciation of bottling machinery	✓		
Depreciation of sales staff's cars			✓
Attendance at a trade exhibition			✓
Office heating and lighting		✓	
Sales staff salaries			✓

1.9

	Production ('factory') costs		Non-production ('warehouse & office') costs		
	Direct Costs	Indirect Costs	Administration Indirect Costs	Selling and Distribution Indirect Costs	Finance Indirect Costs
MATERIALS	3	9	11	12	
LABOUR	2	5	10	8	
EXPENSES		1	7	4	6

1.10

	True	False
• Budgets can never be used as a source of data for historical costs.	✓	
• Information to help with future costs can come from inside and outside the organisation.	✓	
• Future costs are impossible to estimate.		✓
• Financial accounting records and the documents that back up these records are a good source of data for historic costs.	✓	
• If you have a firm quotation from a supplier this is a good source of data for current costs.	✓	
• The number of products that the business forecasts to sell is a good source of data for estimating future income.	✓	
• Costing can only be used for manufacturing businesses, not the service industry.		✓
• Financial accounts can provide a reliable source of data for future costs.		✓
• When costing a future product the labour cost may need to be estimated by using planned labour rates and expected times to make the product.	✓	
• The production level that is planned for is not relevant for costing purposes.		✓

CHAPTER 2: COST CENTRES AND COST BEHAVIOUR

2.1 (b)

2.2

Transaction	Code
Sales in Beachside shop	B100
Cost of paying wages of shop staff at Clifftop	C300
Purchase of new display shelving for Beachside	B900
Purchase of goods for resale at Clifftop shop	C200
Cost of electricity at Clifftop shop	C400
Cost of paying wages of company administrator	A300

2.3

Cost	Code
• wages of drivers	B100
• straight-line depreciation of vehicles	C200
• fuel for vehicles	A100
• rent of premises	C200
• wages of maintenance staff	B200
• advanced driving courses	C200

2.4

Transaction	Code
• Sales invoice showing the sale of £14,750 of academic textbooks to Orton Book Wholesalers Limited	20/420
• Printer's bill of £22,740 for printing sports books	50/110
• Payroll summary showing overtime of £840 last month in the children's book section	40/220
• Payment of £1,540 for advertising sports books in the magazine 'Sport Today'	50/370
• Telephone bill of £1,200 for the administration department	60/340
• Royalties of £88,245 paid to children's book authors	40/310
• Sales invoice showing the sale of £1,890 of novels to the Airport Bookshop	30/410

2.5

Transaction	Code
• Wages of the carpenter who assembles the doors	112
• Sandpaper	221
• Saw sharpening service	123
• Wages of the cleaner who works in the door sanding and polishing section	222
• Office telephone costs	323
• Wood for manufacturing doors	111
• Wages of office worker	322

2.6

	True	False
• Variable costs always include a time period cost		✓
• Fixed costs are based on a time period and the amount does not depend on output	✓	
• Semi-variable costs change directly with changes in the level of activity		✓

2.7

	True	False
• A variable cost is based on a unit of output and is the same for each one	✓	
• A fixed cost changes with changes in the level of activity		✓
• A semi-variable cost is based on a combination of a time period cost and a per unit cost	✓	

2.8

Costs	Fixed	Variable
• Rent of premises	✓	
• Labour paid per unit produced		✓
• Staff salaries	✓	
• Packaging materials for goods produced		✓

2.9

Costs	Fixed	Variable
• Insurance of vehicles	✓	
• Heating and lighting	✓	
• Materials used in production		✓
• Bonus paid to production workers for each extra unit of output		✓

2.10

Costs	Fixed	Variable	Semi-variable
• Factory rates	✓		
• Power for saw and sanders in factory (charged per unit of electricity)		✓	
• Factory supervisors' wages (paid a time rate plus a production-based bonus)			✓
• Wood used in the production process		✓	
• Telephone (charged at a flat rate plus an amount per call)			✓
• Office rent	✓		
• Polish for finishing doors		✓	
• Delivery drivers' pay (paid a time rate plus a bonus per door delivered)			✓
• Factory lighting	✓		
• Wages of production staff who are paid according to the number of doors they make		✓	
• Salary of marketing manager	✓		

2.11

Output (units)	Fixed Costs	Variable Costs	Total Costs	Unit Cost
1,000	£30,000	£20,000	£50,000	£50
1,500	£30,000	£30,000	£60,000	£40
2,000	£30,000	£40,000	£70,000	£35
3,000	£30,000	£60,000	£90,000	£30

2.12

Output (units)	Fixed Costs	Variable Costs	Total Costs	Unit Cost
2,000	£12,000	£ 4,000	£16,000	£8
3,000	£12,000	£ 6,000	£18,000	£6
4,000	£12,000	£ 8,000	£20,000	£5
6,000	£12,000	£12,000	£24,000	£4

2.13

Output (units)	Fixed Costs	Variable Costs	Total Costs	Unit Cost
500	£8,000	£ 2,000	£10,000	£20
1,000	£8,000	£ 4,000	£12,000	£12
2,000	£8,000	£ 8,000	£16,000	£ 8
4,000	£8,000	£16,000	£24,000	£ 6

2.14

	Total cost	Unit cost
Material	£125,000	£ 5
Labour	£100,000	£ 4
Overheads	£ 50,000	£ 2
Total	£275,000	£11

2.15

	Total cost	Unit cost
Material	£300,000	£10
Labour	£240,000	£ 8
Overheads	£ 90,000	£ 3
Total	£630,000	£21

CHAPTER 3: INVENTORY VALUATION AND THE MANUFACTURING ACCOUNT

3.1

Inventory item and organisation	Classification
Wood held by a door manufacturer	raw materials
Flour held by a cake manufacturer	raw materials
Cakes awaiting icing held by a cake manufacturer	work in progress
Doors awaiting sanding and polishing held by a door manufacturer	work in progress
Flour held by a flour miller	finished goods
Wheat held by a flour miller	raw materials
Screws held by a screw manufacturer	finished goods
Screws held by a door manufacturer	raw materials

3.2

Characteristic	FIFO	LIFO	AVCO
• Issues of inventory are valued at the weighted average cost of purchases			✓
• Inventory is valued at the oldest purchase costs		✓	
• Issues of inventory are valued at the most recent purchase prices		✓	
• Inventory is valued at the weighted average cost of purchases			✓
• Inventory is valued at the most recent purchase costs	✓		
• Issues of inventory are valued at the oldest purchase prices	✓		

138 introduction to costing tutorial

3.3

	True	False
• FIFO costs issues of inventory in the same order in which it was received	✓	
• FIFO values closing inventory based on the oldest purchase prices		✓
• LIFO costs issues of inventory at the oldest purchase prices		✓
• LIFO values closing inventory at the average cost of purchases		✓
• AVCO costs issues of inventory at the most recent purchase prices		✓
• AVCO values closing inventory at the weighted average cost of purchases	✓	

3.4 (d)

3.5 (a)

3.6 (b)

3.7 (d)

3.8

FIFO	
LIFO	
AVCO	✓

3.9

Method	Cost of issue on 26 February	Closing inventory value at 28 February
FIFO	£2,300	£4,400
LIFO	£2,900	£3,800
AVCO	£2,580	£4,120

3.10

Method	Cost of issue on 22 January	Closing inventory value at 31 January
FIFO	£1,600	£7,700
LIFO	£2,000	£7,300
AVCO	£1,800	£7,500

3.11 (a) FIFO

Receipts			Issues			Balance		
Quantity (units)	Cost per unit	Total cost	Quantity (units)	Value per unit	Total value	Quantity (units)	Value per unit	Total value
						2,000	£2.02	£4,040
10,000	£2.20	£22,000				2,000	£2.02	£4,040
						10,000	£2.20	£22,000
						12,000		£26,040
			2,000	£2.02	£4,040			
			6,000	£2.20	£13,200			
			8,000		£17,240	4,000	£2.20	£8,800

(b) LIFO

Receipts			Issues			Balance		
Quantity (units)	Cost per unit	Total cost	Quantity (units)	Value per unit	Total value	Quantity (units)	Value per unit	Total value
						2,000	£2.02	£4,040
10,000	£2.20	£22,000				2,000	£2.02	£4,040
						10,000	£2.20	£22,000
						12,000		£26,040
						2,000	£2.02	£4,040
						2,000	£2.20	£4,400
			8,000	£2.20	£17,600	4,000		£8,440

(c) AVCO

Receipts			Issues			Balance		
Quantity (units)	Cost per unit	Total cost	Quantity (units)	Value per unit	Total value	Quantity (units)	Value per unit	Total value
						2,000	£2.02	£4,040
10,000	£2.20	£22,000				12,000	£2.17	£26,040
			8,000	£2.17	£17,360	4,000	£2.17	£8,680

3.12

	£		£
DIRECT COST	79,000	Opening inventory of raw materials	13,000
Opening inventory of raw materials	13,000	Purchases of raw materials	47,000
Direct labour	30,000	Closing inventory of raw materials	11,000
Closing inventory of finished goods	14,000	DIRECT MATERIALS USED	49,000
COST OF GOODS SOLD	93,000	Direct labour	30,000
Purchases of raw materials	47,000	DIRECT COST	79,000
Opening inventory of finished goods	15,000	Manufacturing overheads	20,000
MANUFACTURING COST	99,000	MANUFACTURING COST	99,000
Closing inventory of work in progress	19,000	Opening inventory of work in progress	12,000
Opening inventory of work in progress	12,000	Closing inventory of work in progress	19,000
Closing inventory of raw materials	11,000	COST OF GOODS MANUFACTURED	92,000
DIRECT MATERIALS USED	49,000	Opening inventory of finished goods	15,000
Manufacturing overheads	20,000	Closing inventory of finished goods	14,000
COST OF GOODS MANUFACTURED	92,000	COST OF GOODS SOLD	93,000

3.13

	£		£
Closing inventory of finished goods	32,000	Opening inventory of raw materials	15,000
COST OF GOODS SOLD	178,000	Purchases of raw materials	85,000
Manufacturing overheads	38,000	Closing inventory of raw materials	18,000
Opening inventory of raw materials	15,000	DIRECT MATERIALS USED	82,000
DIRECT MATERIALS USED	82,000	Direct labour	55,000
Opening inventory of work in progress	26,000	DIRECT COST	137,000
Direct labour	55,000	Manufacturing overheads	38,000
MANUFACTURING COST	175,000	MANUFACTURING COST	175,000
Opening inventory of finished goods	37,000	Opening inventory of work in progress	26,000
COST OF GOODS MANUFACTURED	173,000	Closing inventory of work in progress	28,000
Purchases of raw materials	85,000	COST OF GOODS MANUFACTURED	173,000
Closing inventory of work in progress	28,000	Opening inventory of finished goods	37,000
DIRECT COST	137,000	Closing inventory of finished goods	32,000
Closing inventory of raw materials	18,000	COST OF GOODS SOLD	178,000

CHAPTER 4: LABOUR COSTS

4.1 (b)

4.2 (d)

4.3 (a)

4.4

	True	False
• Indirect labour costs cannot be identified with the product or service produced	✓	
• Direct labour costs paid on a time-rate basis do not vary directly with the level of activity	✓	
• Indirect labour costs include the wages of office staff	✓	
• Direct labour costs paid on a piecework basis remain fixed at all levels of output		✓
• Indirect labour costs are a variable cost		✓
• Direct labour costs include the wages of factory supervisors		✓

4.5

Payment method	Time-rate	Piecework	Time-rate plus bonus
• Assured amount of pay for time worked, but no extra pay for efficient working	✓		
• Assured amount of pay for time worked, plus possible extra pay based on output			✓
• No assured amount of pay, but no limit on earnings as pay based on the production of employees		✓	

4.6

Payment method	Time-rate	Piecework	Time-rate plus bonus
• Each unit of production has the same labour cost and payment is made only for productive work		✓	
• Both the employee and the business know in advance how much will be paid	✓		
• When the employee works harder than expected an additional payment is made above the time-rate			✓

4.7

Worker	Hours worked	Basic wage	Overtime	Gross wage
J Cassidy	38	£408	£64	£472
P Olinski	40	£408	£96	£504

4.8

Worker	Units produced in week	Gross wage
T Theaker	344	£430
K Panayi	428	£535

4.9

Worker	Hours worked	Units produced	Basic wage	Bonus	Gross wage
N Allen	32	284	£352	£14	£366
T Chalabi	36	312	£396	£12	£408
A McCall	40	310	£440	£0	£440

4.10

Employee number	Payment methods		
	(a)	(b)	(c)
1	£387	£418	£425
2	£315	£380	£375
3	£351	£285	£380*
4	£375	£399	£410

* no bonus

4.11

Employee	Basic wage or piecework	Overtime or bonus	Gross wage
John Evans (carpenter) – worked 42 hours – paid £10 per hour – overtime at £15 per hour	£400	£30	£430
Vikram Singh (door polisher) – 12 doors polished – paid £35 per door polished	£420	£0	£420
Julian Winstone (part time cleaner) – worked 12 hours – paid £6.50 per hour	£78	£0	£78
Sara Lewinski (office worker) – paid £350 per week	£350	£0	£350

4.12

Employee	Basic pay	Overtime or bonus	Total pay	Code
Jane Buchan	£432	£48	£480	112
Louis Chowski	£432	£64	£496	112
Jim Wright	£500	£80	£580	312
John Rogers	£420	£0	£420	222

4.13

Employee	Basic pay	Overtime	Total pay	Code
Bill Brown	£304	£0	£304	112
Sheila Williams	£440	£66	£506	222
Sonja Patel	£430	£0	£430	122

CHAPTER 5: PROVIDING INFORMATION AND USING SPREADSHEETS

5.1

Element	Total Cost (20,000 units)	Unit Cost
Materials	£300,000	£15
Labour	£40,000	£2
Expenses	£60,000	£3
Total	£400,000	£20

5.2

	10,000 units		15,000 units	
	Total Cost	Unit Cost	Total Cost	Unit Cost
Materials	£80,000	£8	£120,000	£8
Labour	£50,000	£5	£75,000	£5
Fixed Costs	£60,000	£6	£60,000	£4
Total	£190,000	£19	£255,000	£17

5.3

Element	Unit Cost
Material	£5
Labour	£4
Overheads	£2
Total	£11

5.4

Element	Unit Cost
Material	£5
Labour	£6
Overheads	£4
Total	£15

5.5

	True	False
• An adverse variance means budgeted costs are greater than actual costs		✓
• A variance is the difference between budgeted and actual cost	✓	

5.6

	True	False
• A favourable variance means budgeted costs are less than actual costs		✓
• If actual costs are greater than budgeted costs the variance is adverse	✓	

5.7

Cost Type	Budget £	Actual £	Variance	Adverse	Favourable
Direct Materials	45,400	50,200	£4,800	✓	
Direct Labour	28,700	28,200	£500		✓
Production Overheads	19,300	20,200	£900	✓	
Administration Overheads	6,800	6,700	£100		✓
Selling and Distribution Overheads	8,700	9,200	£500	✓	

5.8

Cost Type	Budget £	Actual £	Variance	Adverse	Favourable
Direct Materials	15,400	14,900	£500		✓
Direct Labour	20,300	21,200	£900	✓	
Production Overheads	11,100	10,700	£400		✓
Administration Overheads	7,600	7,800	£200	✓	
Selling and Distribution Overheads	4,900	4,600	£300		✓

5.9

Cost Type	Budget	Variance	Adverse/ Favourable	Significant	Not Significant
Direct Materials	£40,000	£2,500	Adverse	✓	
Direct Labour	£27,500	£1,250	Favourable		✓
Production Overheads	£21,000	£1,000	Adverse		✓
Administration Overheads	£7,500	£500	Adverse	✓	
Selling and Distribution Overheads	£6,500	£750	Favourable	✓	

5.10

Cost Type	Budget	Variance	Adverse/ Favourable	Significant	Not Significant
Direct Materials	£84,000	£8,000	Adverse		✓
Direct Labour	£53,000	£2,500	Favourable		✓
Production Overheads	£26,500	£3,000	Adverse	✓	
Administration Overheads	£12,500	£1,500	Adverse	✓	
Selling and Distribution Overheads	£15,500	£1,000	Favourable		✓

5.11

Cost Type	Budget £	Actual £	Variance	Adverse/ Favourable	Significant/ Not significant
Direct Materials	68,500	64,200	£4,300	Favourable	Significant
Direct Labour	39,100	40,800	£1,700	Adverse	Not significant
Production Overheads	34,700	33,600	£1,100	Favourable	Not significant
Administration Overheads	45,900	51,000	£5,100	Adverse	Significant
Selling and Distribution Overheads	28,000	25,100	£2,900	Favourable	Significant

5.12

	A	B	C	D	E
1	Number of units	Variable Materials £	Variable Labour £	Fixed Costs £	Total Costs £
2	10,000	80,000	20,000	50,000	=SUM(B2:D2)
3	15,000	120,000	30,000	50,000	=SUM(B3:D3)
4	20,000	160,000	40,000	50,000	=SUM(B4:D4)
5	25,000	200,000	50,000	50,000	=SUM(B5:D5)

Other valid formulas could be used.

5.13

	A	B	C	D	E
1	Number of units	Variable Materials £	Variable Labour £	Fixed Costs £	Total Costs £
2	5,000	=A2*10	=A2*5	=28,000	=SUM(B2:D2)
3	7,500	=A3*10	=A3*5	=28,000	=SUM(B3:D3)
4	10,000	=A4*10	=A4*5	=28,000	=SUM(B4:D4)

Other valid formulas could be used.

5.14

	A	B	C	D	E
1		Budget £	Actual £	Variance £	A /F
2	Income	210,000	206,000	=B2-C2	A
3	Materials	44,500	44,600	=C3-B3	A
4	Labour	63,100	62,000	=B4-C4	F
5	Overheads	70,500	74,300	=C5-B5	A
6	Profit	=B2-B3-B4-B5	=C2-C3-C4-C5	=B6-C6	A

Other valid formulas could be used.

5.15

	A	B	C	D	E	F	G
1		Jo King £	Shelley Beach £	Justin Case £	Cliff Topp £	Section Total £	Average Pay £
2	Basic pay	288	320	296	312	1,216	304
3	Bonus	12	30	24	32	=SUM(B3:E3)	=AVERAGE(B3:E3)
4	Total pay	300	350	320	344	=SUM(B4:E4)	=AVERAGE(B4:E4)
5		%	%	%	%	%	
6	Bonus % of total pay	4	=C3/C4%	=D3/D4%	=E3/E4%	=F3/F4%	

Other valid formulas could be used.

Index

Budget
    definition, 103
    purpose, 103
    standard costs, 104
    variances, 104

Classification of costs
    elements, 9-10
    function, 11
    nature, 11
Coding, uses in costing, 30
Coding systems
    alpha-numeric, 30
    alphabetic, 30
    numeric, 30
Cost behaviour
    calculations, 39-41
    definition, 32
    fixed costs, 33
    identification, 36
    semi-variable costs, 35
    unit cost, 40
    variable costs, 34
Cost centre, 27-28
Cost of goods manufactured, 67
Cost of goods sold, 69
Cost reports
    cost behaviour, 102
    unit cost, 101

Costing system, 2-20
    definition, 3
    sources of data, 6
Costs
    manufacturers, 9-13
    non-manufacturing organisations, 15-16

Direct costs, 11,12,15,67

Elements of cost
    expenses, 10
    labour, 10
    materials, 10

Financial accounting, 4-5
Fixed costs, 33
Functions of cost, 11

Income, 11
Indirect costs, 11,12,15
Inventory (stock)
    finished goods, 53
    raw materials, 53
    valuation, 54-65
    work-in-progress, 53
Inventory (stock) valuation
    AVCO (Average Cost), 56,58
    calculations, 61-65
    characteristics, 59-60

FIFO (First In First Out), 56,57
LIFO (Last In First Out), 56,58
need for valuation, 54
use of valuation, 65-71
Investment centres, 29

Labour costs, 10,82-92
  behaviour, 89-91
  bonus payments, 84
  classification, 87
  direct, 88
  fixed, 89
  indirect, 88
  methods of calculating pay, 83
  overtime rate, 84
  piecework, 85
  semi-variable, 90
  time rate, 83
  variable, 89

Management accounting, 4-6
Manufacturing accounts, 65-71
  cost of goods manufactured, 67
  cost of goods sold, 69
  direct cost, 67
  direct materials used, 66
  manufacturing cost, 67
Materials costs, 10
Manufacturing cost, 67

Nature of costs
  direct costs, 11
  indirect costs, 11

Non-production costs, 12

Overheads, 10,12

Profit centres, 28-29

Semi-variable costs, 35
Sources of costing data
  current cost, 7
  future cost, 7
  historic cost, 7
Spreadsheets, 109-119
  addition, 114
  AUTOSUM function, 116
  AVERAGE function, 117
  basic formulas, 113
  percentages, 117
  presenting information, 111
  sorting data, 119
  subtraction, 115
  SUM function, 116
  terms, 110
Standard costs, 104

Using spreadsheets, 109-119

Variable costs, 34
Variances
  adverse, 104
  calculation of, 105
  favourable, 104
  percentages, 107
  significant variances, 106

for your notes

for your notes

for your notes

for your notes